When a Family
Member Has Dementia

When a Family Member Has Dementia

STEPS TO BECOMING A RESILIENT CAREGIVER ◆

Susan M. McCurry

Foreword by Linda Teri

PRAEGER

Westport, Connecticut
London

Library of Congress Cataloging-in-Publication Data

McCurry, Susan M.
    When a family member has dementia : steps to becoming a resilient
caregiver / Susan M. McCurry ; foreword by Linda Teri.
        p.   cm.
    Includes bibliographical references and index.
    ISBN 0–275–98574–1 (alk. paper)
    1. Dementia.   2. Dementia—Patients—Care.   3. Caregivers.   I. Title.
RC521.M39   2006
    362.196'83—dc22   2005025490

British Library Cataloguing in Publication Data is available.

Library of Congress Catalog Card Number: 2005025490
ISBN: 0–275–98574–1

First published in 2006

Praeger Publishers, 88 Post Road West, Westport, CT 06881
An imprint of Greenwood Publishing Group, Inc.
www.praeger.com

Printed in the United States of America

The paper used in this book complies with the
Permanent Paper Standard issued by the National
Information Standards Organization (Z39.48-1984).

10 9 8 7 6 5 4 3 2 1

To Anne and Craig

There is an appointed time for everything,
A time to weep, and a time to laugh,
A time to mourn, and a time to dance.

Ecclesiastes 3:1, 4

Contents

Foreword

Many years ago, while presenting to a group of professionals and family members interested in learning how to deal with the behavioral problems so common in Alzheimer's disease, I discussed the need to slow down and be aware of how we communicate—to treat the person with dementia as we would like to be treated. On one hand, this concept is so critical that it needs to be said, and said strongly. On the other hand, this seems to me such a fundamental act of kindness and respect that it should be obvious and easy to achieve. Because of that, I made the comment, "This isn't rocket science; it's common sense—basic human compassion." At the end of my presentation, as is often the case, a number of people came up to discuss what I had said or to ask an additional question. One gentleman, in particular, hung about the back and waited for everyone else to finish. When it was his turn, he addressed me in a very strong, authoritative voice. "Young lady," he said, "you are wrong when you say this isn't rocket science—to say that what you do is simple." I immediately went into full alert, concerned I had somehow insulted this gentleman or seemed uncaring to my audience. He continued, "I worked for NASA for over 30 years. I *am* a rocket scientist. Rocket science is all equations and numbers, and predictable. What you do is much harder. You deal with people. People are unpredictable. Don't undersell yourself. God bless you." I have never forgotten that gentleman or his message.

If you are caring for a person with a chronic debilitating disease, such as Alzheimer's or a related dementia, do not undersell yourself. You have a hard, complicated, and frequently unpredictable job. The daily challenges of care cause us to draw upon reserves and skills we often do not know we have until we need them. You also have the joys inherent in the human condition—love, laughter, and hope. The unexpected rewards of improving the life of someone we care about and the joys we could not have anticipated are often overlooked because we are barraged with information about all the bad things that can happen in this debilitating disease. Persons with dementia can experience joy and love. They can have good days, and you, their caregiver, can be the person most likely to help this happen. Plus, the magic of caregiving means that the more good days they have, the more good days you have as well.

Dr. McCurry brings to the caregiving community this book of hope. By presenting glimpses of the caregivers she has worked with over her years of clinical work, she shows the rich diversity of possibilities. She illustrates how things can improve, as well as how to cope with those times when it feels like things can only get worse. For caregivers just embarking on this mission, Dr. McCurry's compassion shines through. She will help you understand the disease process as well as how to deal with it. For experienced caregivers, whether family or friend, Dr. McCurry's insights may bring new ideas to old problems.

I have had the privilege of working with thousands of caregivers and hundreds of clinicians. Dr. McCurry stands out in the array of those who spend their lives trying to improve the human condition. She is not a rocket scientist. She is a caregiver—and a good one. I hope her book helps you appreciate the rewards of caregiving and strengthens your ability to provide the best care you possibly can.

Linda Teri, PhD
University of Washington

Preface

I have long felt that persons who live with a dementing illness—caregivers and care-recipients alike—are the unsung heroes of our modern day. Dementia is greatly misunderstood. It was not so long ago that the changes and symptoms associated with dementia were considered a kind of mental illness, shameful, and something to be hidden. Even today, because there are so few external signs of disease that accompany the behavioral changes in dementia, there is a tendency to blame the affected individual. We blame their personalities, their histories, their motivation, and their willpower. We find their problems to be ugly and disturbing, and remove ourselves so we do not have to feel the discomfort that being around them provokes in us. No wonder caregivers become isolated and so ferociously protective of their loved ones!

However, those of us who work closely with persons with dementia and their caregivers see a different picture. We see the incredible dignity with which patients face their diagnosis. We see the ingenuity and determination with which caregivers advocate for their loved ones. Not that caring for someone with dementia is always easy or pleasant. I have also seen the anxiety, grief, exhaustion, and despair that dementia can create in both the caregiver and the care-recipient. Nevertheless, hidden behind the dark face of dementia are men and women of courage who have been loving parents, devoted spouses, faithful children, friends, neighbors, and workmates. Sparkles of wit and intelligence and unexpected selfness shine through gaps in memory and confusion. These elders may not always remember what they had for breakfast, but they still have something to teach us.

People sometimes ask how I can do this work. I grew up in the company of older adults—men and women who were my parents' peers but were the age of many of my friends' grandparents. In my twenties and thirties, I involved myself in volunteer work that frequently meant spending time with the aged: visiting nursing homes, providing chore services to elderly church members, and working as a hospice volunteer. I spent these formative years talking and listening to people with a variety of cognitive impairments, including my own father, who suffered from a series of small strokes and ultimately a brain tumor toward the end of his life. Dementia, in its many intensities and varieties, was familiar to me, and not a fearsome thing but rather part of the diversity of personalities and lives of those around me.

When I became a clinical psychologist, I naturally gravitated toward training experiences and jobs working with older adults, many of whom could tell vivid stories about their childhoods, but could not recognize the person they were living with now. I have never found this work to be depressing. It is an incomparable privilege to be allowed to share the doubts, uplifts, sorrows, and laughter of persons with dementia and of the loved ones who are their caregivers. Every situation is different. Beneath every dementia syndrome is a real person, someone with strengths and weaknesses that are now attenuated or exaggerated by their disease, to be sure, but nevertheless a human being who desperately wants to be understood and treated with dignity and respect. Within every caregiver is a person who, more than anything, wants to help. He or she may not have a clue how to go about doing that. They may be frustrated, exhausted, discouraged, confused, and afraid that you will judge them, but they are always doing the best they can and always hoping to learn something that will help them do a better job.

This book is for them, the dementia patients and caregivers who have challenged, touched, and inspired me throughout the course of my life. There have been many times when I have walked out of a clinic session feeling that I should be paying the family that just spent an hour in my office, pouring out its life, rather than the other way around. Caregivers find surprising ways to flourish in the midst of suffering, to "make lemons into lemonade," or, at the very least, to find peace in their difficult role. This book is an attempt to weave the lessons of hope and gratitude that I have received into a simple, easy-to-remember formula for managing dementia-related behavior problems, one that is useful, whether caregivers are coping with the very early stages of memory loss, or have been living with a dementia patient for many years. Over the next few decades, as unprecedented numbers of the baby-boomer generation become caregivers and care recipients, we will need to be able to draw upon the resilience and wisdom of the dementia heroes who have already walked this path before us.

Acknowledgments

When you write your first book, it is a lot like delivering your first child. No matter how many people you talk to, no matter how many books on the subject you read, you are never fully prepared for how all-encompassing and challenging the process is going to be. What did I do with all that time I must have had before I started writing a book? However, just as children bring new friendships, new discoveries, and new growth, so has this book done the same for me. It is absolutely the case that I could not have even begun, let alone finished, the book without the help of the many people who gave of themselves so generously from beginning to end of its creation.

I gratefully acknowledge the caregiver who said to me one day, two years ago, "Have you ever considered writing a book?" Her question was a gift of grace, without which I would have never gotten started. I would like to thank my agent, Stan Wakefield, who dropped into my life unexpectedly, offered unbelievable enthusiasm and motivation to get the initial proposal written, and ultimately provided the contact with Praeger that has led to this book's publication. During the project's early stages, David Barash, Bobbie Berkowitz, Marie-Annette Brown, Wendy Lustbader, and Heather Young graciously shared their time and book publication stories with me. It was enormously helpful to hear others' experiences, and to also hear them say, "Go for it!" Wingate Packard, a fellow mom and editor par excellence, reacted to my early drafts with thoughtfulness and good sense. This book is much better for her hard work and perspective.

I would like to acknowledge Elizabeth Potenza, my editor at Praeger, who believed in this project and in me, an unknown first author, sufficiently to give me the chance to make it happen. Elizabeth advocated for me at points of conflict and confusion. I am very grateful she was there.

I must extend my thanks to all the friends, colleagues, and caregivers who listened to my ideas, shared their own, and read early drafts of this manuscript, giving me much-needed support, inspiration, and suggestions for change. Although it would be impossible to mention everyone by name, Maureen Brinck-Lund, Julie Cleveland, Martha DuHamel, Steven Graybar, Marie Kirkman, Barbara Kohlenberg, Eric Larson, Sheila O'Connell, Ed Price, Meredith Pfanschmidt, Linda Pinsky, Edward Schau, Darrell Thomas, and Joanne Webb should be acknowledged. Victoria Ries helped me stay in touch with the real spirit and motivation that underlies this book, throughout the many ups and downs of its preparation. Particular credit must be given to Rebecca Logsdon and Linda Teri, both outstanding geropsychologists and wonderful human beings. I could have never even conceived this project without my years of collaboration with them. It is impossible to emphasize enough how much they have influenced and helped me throughout my career, including while I was writing this book. It must be acknowledged that the heart of this book is as much theirs as mine.

My deepest gratitude goes to my husband, Chris, and son, Ian, who put up with many nights and weekends where the book demanded my time and attention. They believed in me, they love me, and it is hard to imagine how I could have done it without them.

Lastly, I must acknowledge the many persons with dementia and their caregivers who have shared their stories and lives with me over the years. I owe a great debt to the individuals whose stories grace these pages. In gratitude to their generosity, I have taken care to protect their identity by changing not only names but also details of their problems, relationships, and life circumstances. Frequently, I weaved together multiple stories to illustrate a point. If you believe you recognize your friends, neighbors, and family members, it is only because the challenges, sorrows, and triumphs described in this book are universal to the caregiver's world.

Section I

THE PROBLEM:

Dementia Caregiving Is Hard!

Caring for a person with dementia is a difficult and often overwhelming task. More and more people are facing this challenge. An estimated 360,000 persons are diagnosed with Alzheimer's disease or a related dementia every year, and this number will increase as the population ages. Over 70 percent of these demented individuals live at home and are cared for by family and friends. After the initial flurry of activity and information dissemination when a dementia diagnosis is first made, caregivers are left to figure out on their own how to take care of a person who is increasingly volatile, stubborn, confused, and dependent. Caregivers often feel very alone.

Dementia presents a variety of challenges to caregivers. In addition to the inevitable decline in memory and physical function, the vast majority of persons with dementia develop one or more troublesome behavior problems such as depression, fearfulness, sleep disturbances, suspiciousness and paranoia, or physical aggression at some point in their disease. Behavioral challenges in dementia are highly idiosyncratic; no two individuals are alike, and interventions that work well with one person are often ineffective with another. Another challenge caregivers face is that dementia is by nature a changing or evolving situation. No sooner is one problem resolved than a new one appears. One day the demented individual responds easily to reason, and the next day, is resistant to any attempt to influence his or her behavior. Family members are often divided over the best way to handle the demented individual because he or she acts differently with each of them. These behavioral inconsistencies in a person who looks perfectly healthy are common in dementia, but can make caring for that person extremely challenging.

Health-care professionals encourage caregivers to be consistent, but how is that possible when the person being cared for behaves so differently from day to day? Caregivers become "stuck": either unable to figure out how best to help their loved ones, or unable to consistently implement positive practices that they know might improve the situation.

Added to the daily variability is the relentless nature of dementia care. Persons diagnosed with Alzheimer's disease live, on average, seven to ten years after diagnosis, and most of those years will be spent at home. As the disease progresses, there are changes in the kinds of behavior problems exhibited by demented persons. In the beginning, the person makes many mistakes that come from simply forgetting: bills go unpaid (or are paid twice!), appointments are missed, parked cars are misplaced, and pots are left to boil dry on the stove. Just about the time you figure out how to work around memory lapses, new changes in personality, social judgment, and dramatic mood swings may appear, many of which are triggered by ordinary routines and self-care activities such as dressing, showering, and taking medications. Caregivers once accustomed to an efficient lifestyle and busy pace now find that everything takes more time, and anything can happen. It is no wonder that many caregivers feel ineffective and helpless. They are doing the best they can, yet they feel like Sisyphus pushing a rock up a hill, pushing against the progressive deterioration in someone they love, only to have their efforts come crashing back down each time a new problem emerges or a previously effective intervention no longer works.

If you are reading this book, chances are you are a caregiver, in one form or another. You may be a wife, husband, daughter, or son helping a family member whom you live with and love. You may be a neighbor or a friend, watching out for an older man or woman down the street who is struggling to stay independent in his or her own home. Or you may be a health-care provider, wondering how best to help the person sitting across from you, who has just been told that his or her spouse, parent, or sibling has progressive dementia. For all of you, the task is the same: you must learn to trust your instincts, to be flexible, and to believe that you have within you great wisdom and creativity that will guide you in your role as caregiver. In this book, you will hear how other caregivers have faced the daily challenges of caring for someone with dementia, and you will find some specific suggestions for overcoming common dementia-related mood and behavior problems. You will learn what the latest research in the field of aging has to say about the strategies and concepts presented in the book. However, the focus of the book will be on helping you develop creative and respectful solutions individualized to your unique situation. In the process, you will discover new opportunities for personal growth, and, hopefully, new dimensions to your relationship with your loved one. This is a book designed not to help you just survive being a caregiver, but to help you thrive as you provide help and care to someone who needs you. You can do more than you think you can for yourself and for the person with dementia. You can begin to practice the art of resilience.

Chapter 1

WHY RESILIENCE MATTERS ◆

The word "resilience" is derived from the Latin verb *resilire*, which means "to spring back." *The Random House Dictionary of the English Language* defines resilience as elasticity, "the power or ability to return to the original form...after being bent, compressed, or stretched."[1] Resilience is adaptation—an ability to accommodate, and to keep moving and trying new strategies in response to constantly changing circumstances. Researchers interested in resilience have sometimes used the analogy of a coiled wire as one way of thinking about it. Imagine such a coil pressed into the bottom of a jack-in-the-box. The coiled wire is very strong; it can rebound many times after being compressed down by the lid of the jack-in-the-box. The potential to spring back into shape is part of the wire's nature, regardless of whether it is acting "springy" at the moment or in the current environment. Over time, the resilience or elasticity of the coiled wire may change as a result of age or use. However, the natural tendency of the wire will always be to return to its original shape once the compression is released.

Many caregivers can relate to the metaphor of being pressed down and stretched out of shape, but it is harder to think about springing back to normal. Settling into life with someone who has dementia can be very bewildering. For most of us, there is nothing in our life experience to prepare us for helping someone who is convinced they are perfectly fine but cannot remember what they did or said fifteen minutes ago. The wife of fifty years is devastated the first morning her husband does not recognize her. The adult daughter who spends a week replacing identification and credit cards after mom loses her wallet is dismayed when the wallet turns up in her mother's freezer, hidden behind the ice cream. The man eating in an upscale restaurant is horrified when his wife stands up and begins taking off her panty hose in front of the other patrons because she is hot. Most perplexing of all, one hour or one day later—often when other family or health-care professionals are called in to evaluate the situation—the person may be acting completely normal, and the caregiver feels like a fool and is furious with everyone.

It is difficult for the average caregiver to figure out how to rebound from such unpredictability and unexpected demands. You may feel like you are trapped in that jack-in-the-box and there is no way to open the lid. Caregivers who feel trapped, who have lost touch with their inner resilience, can easily fall into two common, but ineffective, patterns.[2] The first of these I call Resigned Caregivers, who sacrifice all their personal needs to assume the caregiving role. Loving and well intentioned, these caregivers are often reluctant to ask for help from family and friends. Over time, they can become isolated, exhausted, sick, and often clinically depressed. The second common pattern is the Resentful Caregiver, who feels he or she has gotten stuck with a bad job no one else wanted. These caregivers cannot believe that the person with dementia is not capable of doing more things for himself, and they view mood and behavior problems as deliberate misconduct. They may even question the dementia diagnosis. Such caregivers can become neglectful, verbally or physically abusive, and a drain on the health-care system because they think doctors should be able to solve this problem. Caregivers who are caught up in resignation or resentment, or some combination of the two, have a very difficult time negotiating the challenges of caring for an older adult with dementia. Let us look at some examples of what can happen.

Jacqueline loved her mom. Both her parents had lived with Jacqueline, a single, successful health-care professional, for over twenty years. It had not been easy, but Jacqueline's two siblings had families of their own, and they lived far away—it just made sense for Jacqueline to take care of her parents. After her dad died, mom did pretty well for a couple of years, but eventually, increasing memory problems, physical frailty, and poor judgment made it difficult to leave her alone. Jacqueline withdrew money from her retirement account to remodel her house so mom would not have to go up and down stairs. She hired in-home help so she could be at the office during the day, but a series of aides quit or had to be let go because her mom disliked having strangers in the home. Jacqueline's accountant informed her that all this outflow of cash was pushing back the date when she would be able to quit working, which was a problem because Jacqueline was being pressured to retire now as she was taking so much time off from work to care for her mom. To save money, Jacqueline stopped going to the theater, gave up her gym membership, and canceled her annual vacation with friends. All this might have been worth it if mom had seemed appreciative, but instead, all Jacqueline heard was criticism and complaints.

One day, while Jacqueline was trying to transfer her mom out of bed, her mom fell and broke a hip. After much soul searching, Jacqueline decided to move her mom from the rehab hospital into a nearby nursing home. She visited several times a day for months to make sure mom was getting the best care possible, hired personal aides to be there at meal times to help out, reported nursing staff who did not seem to be doing a good job, and oversaw her mom's medical management. When Jacqueline's brother came to visit his mom at the nursing home, she was crying, and begged him to take her away since no one ever came to visit her; she said she would prefer to die alone in her own bed. Jacqueline's brother was furious, and called his sister on the phone to blame her for their mother's fall and abandonment. This left Jacqueline so distraught she could barely drag herself out of bed for the next several days.

Jacqueline is a classic example of a resigned caregiver. After her dad's death, Jacqueline wound up being the primary caregiver for her increasingly demented mother. She had a very real love for, and commitment to, her parents. Her mistake was trying to do so much of it alone. She assumed sole responsibility for her mother's care, even though she had siblings and other family who could have been more involved. Her reluctance to ask for help arose in part from family and cultural expectations that assumed the unmarried daughter should care for her aging parents. It also was easier just to do everything herself. Jacqueline hated asking her siblings for money, and hated having to justify her decisions about mom's care to family members who were far away and did not really understand what was going on. But this freedom from interdependence on others came at a great cost. By the time I met Jacqueline, her job and retirement security were in jeopardy, her weight and blood pressure were skyrocketing, and she was very depressed and bitter over both her mother's and brother's lack of gratitude. Despite all this, the precipitant for Jacqueline coming into my clinic was her decision to try to bring her mother back home. She wanted help figuring out how to implement her plan.

In other cases, a dementia diagnosis comes as a shock that is hard to accept. Caregivers who are caught by surprise, or who believe that their loved one's diagnosis signals an end to all their future hopes and dreams, are more vulnerable to feelings of resentment, as in the story below.

Alison and Joe were married two years ago. Both were widowed, after long, happy marriages to their first partners. It seemed like a great match; their adult children were happy for them, they had enough money to travel, and both were in excellent health for their advanced years. Two months after the wedding, however, Joe invested a large sum of money in a fly-by-night business venture after receiving a telemarketer's call. Soon, other financial misadventures followed. He closed out a checking account, but could not explain where the money had gone. Several credit cards were run up with purchases they did not need and donations to charities that

Alison had never heard of. When Alison questioned Joe about these matters, he became angry, accusing her of not trusting his judgment. One night, Joe did not come home after visiting his daughter's house. The police found him in the next town, twenty miles away—confused, hungry, and frightened.

Alison finally insisted Joe see a doctor, and learned that Joe was suspected of having Alzheimer's disease. Furious, she later confided to me, "This was not what I intended for the rest of my life. I would *never* have married Joe if I had known he had Alzheimer's! No one gave me any hints that he had been having problems, and he hid them from me until after the wedding. I'm exhausted from worrying about him, and my doctor says I'm making myself sick with the stress. If he doesn't pull himself together and start working with me, I'm going to leave and let his kids deal with it. But I worry if I do that, what will happen to Joe?"

Alison is a good example of a resentful caregiver. She had reached a time in her life when she felt she was entitled to relax and enjoy herself. She felt little loyalty sticking with this new marriage if it meant she was going to spend years taking care of a demented husband. She felt betrayed by both Joe and his kids. Even though Joe had not been told he might have Alzheimer's disease until Alison took him to the doctor, she was certain that there must have been early warning signs, and felt that someone in his family should have pointed these out to her. Joe's social and verbal abilities were quite intact, and he was still held in high esteem in the business community. It infuriated Alison that Joe could act so normally at a dinner party but then be so impossible to reason with about his continuing financial fiascoes. Alison was not a bad person. She was simply caught up in a whirlwind of shattered dreams, confusion over Joe's inconsistent behavior, exhaustion, and fear of what would happen next. She wished Joe well, but still felt trapped and alone. If things were this terrible now, how would she possibly manage when Joe got worse? Alison wanted to escape.

TURNING THE TIDE TOWARD RESILIENT CAREGIVING

If you recognize yourself in the stories of Jacqueline and Alison, do not despair! You are not alone and you are not to blame. Resignation and resentment are common reactions in caregivers of persons with dementia. Both Jacqueline and Alison felt that they were trapped, that they had nowhere to go and no good options. Both were highly competent individuals who were extremely frustrated at their inability to take control of a situation that seemed to be spiraling out of hand. They were physically worn out and socially isolated. The likely scenarios running through their minds for the future were dreadful.

Resigned and resentful caregivers lose their ability to see any way out of their situation. Unfortunately, they also lose the ability to see their current situation fully.[3] Very real irritations, difficulties, fears, and disappointments all flow into one another so that the equally real moments, hours, and even days that are free of crisis, or even beautiful in some way, are completely overlooked. They are living in their heads and their hearts, but with blinders that obscure much of the world around them. They do not know how to open the lid to that jack-in-the-box and release their own resilient wisdom. If anything, they are at risk to become more rigid and locked-in than ever before, in a desperate bid to try to make their situation more manageable.

Fortunately, there is another path you can take. Every clinician who works with persons who have dementia knows caregivers who are amazing in their ability to figure out what to do to improve the situation, both for themselves and for the person who is receiving care. These caregivers fit a pattern that I call Resilient Caregivers. They come from every age, gender, socioeconomic level, and ethnic background; they can be spouses, adult children, distant relatives, good friends, or paid staff. Despite their apparent diversity, resilient caregivers share some important commonalities. Although they are often caring for someone with significant psychiatric or physical impairment, they are able to detach themselves and not take the person's behavior personally.[4] They maintain a sense of humor. They are aware of the tender moments in their day, and look for the "uplifts" that are part of being a caregiver. They have learned to "pick their battles," so that they know when to push and when to just let it go. They are willing to ask for help. They do things to take care of their own physical and emotional health despite limited time and resources. Mario is one example.

"In the beginning," Mario said, "being a caregiver didn't seem too bad." True, his wife, Elaina, no longer could make his favorite pasta sauce without burning it. She did not do such a great job keeping their little house tidy or keeping the weeds out of the vegetable garden. She could not remember how to sort the laundry, and once poured detergent and bleach into the dryer instead of the washing machine. Little by little, Mario found himself taking on more and more "women's work," but it was OK, better than he had thought it would be. What was hard was seeing his pretty, vivacious Elaina becoming so fearful and suspicious. She accused their grandson of stealing her jewelry. She paced the living room, especially in the evening, and occasionally would try to run out of the house. One night, Mario awakened in his bed to find Elaina standing over him with a sharpened pencil in her hand, pointed at his face. After a brief hospitalization in a geriatric psychiatric unit, Elaina was doing better but she was still often very frightened. She startled when the phone or doorbell rang. She did not want Mario out of her sight, even to use the bathroom. It drove him crazy!

Gradually, however, Mario noticed that as long as someone was at her side, Elaina did pretty well. She was easily distracted and generally cooperative, so long as she was not left alone. He began to take her everywhere. Mario said to me, "I used to be very shy and kept to myself. Elaina was the one who had all the friends and held the family together. But I've changed. I just decided that I wouldn't be able to take care of her unless I started doing things differently. Now, I strike up conversations with everyone. I call up the kids and ask them to come over. It keeps me from feeling so alone. And I laugh a lot more, even at things Elaina does that annoy me. It isn't easy, being with her all the time or finding other people to help, but I remind myself that this is for my Elaina. I try to figure out what makes her happy and then I do that. When I have a bad day, I tell myself to forget it and start over in the morning."

Mario's story illustrates that being resilient does not mean one never feels anxious, resigned, resentful, burdened, or depressed. Rather, the resilient caregiver is one who keeps going and keeps growing, despite very real difficulties. But how does one become resilient? Is resilience a trait you are simply born with, or is it a skill anyone can learn?

THE RESILIENCE ALTERNATIVE

Many researchers do view resilience as a personality trait, something that is more innate than learned.[5] Stress-resilient people are often described as intelligent, optimistic, creative, physically attractive, good at self-regulation, flexible, and high in self-esteem. They have what could be called "emotional stamina": determination, a belief in their own abilities, a sense of humor, and often a faith in God or some higher power that can provide direction and purpose to life. Studies with older adults have found that resilience is associated with good self-rated health, low rates of depression, and independence in daily activities such as shopping and using public transportation. It has been suggested that resilient individuals may have unique neurobiological ways of responding to stress that help them stay positive in difficult situations, avoid overgeneralizing isolated problems to the larger context, and form supportive social attachments more easily.[6]

Perhaps you are saying to yourself, "You're not describing me—I'm not optimistic, attractive, my health isn't very good, and I certainly don't feel very intelligent or competent right now! Does that mean that I am not resilient? Does it mean that I don't have what it takes to deal with the difficult changes that my loved one and I are experiencing right now?" Fortunately, that is not the case. As part of its ongoing "Road to Resilience" public education campaign, the American Psychological Association (APA) has stated that resilience is an ordinary set of behaviors, thoughts, and actions that anyone can learn and develop.[7] Even if you feel stuck right now, you are capable of being resilient. However, you may need to find a way to get more in touch with your inner resilience, which will help you discover new ways to deal with your situation. One way to get in touch with your personal resilience is to think, like Mike does here, about other times and situations in your life that were highly challenging, but in which you nevertheless responded well.

Mike was a highly successful local businessman who was having a very difficult time caring for his demented wife. In talking with him, I learned that Mike had been a World War II hero who survived a mine explosion and subsequent leg amputation. Mike said he got through those early postwar years by focusing on what he could still do, despite his missing leg, rather than thinking about the goals he had to give up because of his injury. He set his mind on learning to walk with a prosthesis, and made new friends who were fellow amputees and could understand his struggles. On days when he felt particularly low, he reminded himself that it could have been worse: he might have lost both legs, or his eyesight. In my meetings with Mike, we talked about whether those strategies he had used to get through the early years after the war might help him now. Mike began to joke that he was his wife's "prosthetic memory," and it helped him to accept previously distasteful tasks like assisting her with brushing teeth and toileting. He started attending an Alzheimer's support group, where he could talk with other caregivers. In the process of doing that, he heard lots of stories that made him appreciate how much worse off things could have been for him at home. Even though he did not always know what to do, Mike came to realize that he was not alone, and that no matter what happened, there was someone he could call to help him figure it out.

Mike's scenario is a good example of how resilience is a dynamic interaction between personal characteristics and the current situation.[8] Mike had a powerful history of acting resiliently in the face of severe stress. However, people do not necessarily react the same way to all stressors. In his past situation, as terrible as the war injury and loss of limb was, once it happened, it was over and Mike had developed new skills to move forward. What he found so difficult in his current situation was that there was no single stressor to move past. He was in an ongoing situation, where the smallest basic chore or self-care activity had the potential to become a repetitive nightmare. It would have been much easier to be resilient, to be optimistic and flexible in a situation where Mike felt more in control of the outcome. With help, however, Mike could begin to see the similarities between what helped him in the past and what could help him now. Resilience is a process of adapting to adversity or stress. It can be learned by anyone at any age, in any situation, and it can become a habit. It is important for caregivers to know and believe this; no matter how difficult or desperate your situation may seem right now, chances are that there are undiscovered choices or opportunities waiting to be considered. There are always possibilities you have not tried.

THE ART OF LEARNING RESILIENCE

Although resilience is an innate capacity that all human beings possess, it takes practice to be good at it. The circumstances of our lives provide the opportunity to practice, and, like any action, the more resilience is practiced, the easier it becomes. Over time, resilient responding becomes a habit. Change is hard, however, and unpredictable change, which is regularly encountered in the life of a dementia caregiver, may be the hardest of all. Left to our own devices, many of us comfortably settle into familiar routines and go through our lives making as few changes as possible. Our resilience skills become like an underexercised muscle: painful to use, clumsy, and slow. When challenges come along that demand flexibility and change, we may be so psychologically out of shape that it seems we are incapable of resilient responding.

Fortunately, it is never too late to learn to do something new, no matter how challenging. Exercise is a good analogy for resilience. I have an older friend who was physically very inactive and overweight for much of his life, until one day he embarked on an exercise and weight-loss program that eventually turned him into a real athlete. It did not happen overnight; it took a couple of years. He had people who supported him, coaches who could teach him tricks to make exercise easier or more effective, and friends who encouraged him and worked out with him, even on days when he felt tired or lazy or discouraged. My friend's accomplishments are not unique; the scientific literature contains countless studies that show it is never too late to begin and benefit from an exercise program.[9] Similarly, it is never too late to build up our emotional stamina: our innate capacity to recover, to bounce back from the shocks, hurts, disappointments, and surprises of life, including being a dementia caregiver. As with exercise, building resilience takes time, and the strategies that work best for you are very personal. You need people to support, teach, and motivate you. You need to start out with little steps and goals; you do not enter a marathon until you can run a mile, and you cannot expect to change a lifetime of habits overnight. You will need to experiment to discover specifically what tools will be most helpful on your personal path to greater resilience. Most important, you will need to practice what you are learning. You will need to develop your resilience "muscles."

Perhaps you are thinking that developing resilience is very different from starting an exercise routine. Is there any evidence that resilience is something that can be learned? Indeed, there is. Case studies in the medical literature describe the way in which individual or family psychotherapy can lead to development of greater resilience, including improved communication, problem-solving abilities, and utilization of appropriate resources for coping with stress and chronic illness.[10] Researchers at Duke University have recently published data showing that treatment for anxiety, in community samples, is associated with self-reported improvements in resilience, with greater reductions in anxiety found in persons with greatest increases in resilience.[11] The Duke findings were based on a relatively small sample, and they do not resolve questions about how resilience develops, or is learned. Nevertheless, the study offers the first empirical evidence that resilience is modifiable. Anyone can develop and nourish their potential for resilience and begin to respond to life in more positive and adaptive ways.

What can you do to help develop your unique resilience potential? One strategy is to think back on your life, as Mike did in the example above, and remember other difficult times you have been through. How have you overcome physical, emotional, or financial adversity in the past? Even if these crises were very different from the challenges you face now with caregiving, remembering what you did to take care of yourself, to get help and take advantage of it, can tell you a lot about the strengths and resources you may be able to use today. A second way might be to rate your personal resilience using a standardized questionnaire developed just for this purpose. The best self-report measure currently available for caregivers is called the Resilience Scale.[12] This scale, which asks you to rate twenty-five items relating to feelings of self-reliance, meaningfulness, and perseverance, has been validated by hundreds of community-dwelling older adults. It has been translated and validated in several languages, and has been specifically used to measure the relationship between resilience, burden, and depression in dementia caregivers. A shortened version of this questionnaire is included as part of an exercise at the end of this chapter.[13]

SUMMARY

There is an old expression, "That which does not kill us, makes us stronger." Virtually all caregivers of persons with dementia have a history of successfully dealing with challenges in their lifetimes, which they bring to their current caregiving role. I have never met caregivers who cannot describe times in their lives when their personal resilience and perseverance carried them through difficult situations. Some caregivers' resilience stories arise from experiences that are common to the aging process: bodies failing, friends and family dying or leaving, or financial resources becoming exhausted. However, younger caregivers, grandchildren or nephews and nieces of the person with dementia, have also frequently described to me experiences from their past that make it possible for them to take on responsibilities that few of their peers can begin to understand. It is not biological age but developmental stage that matters. Erik Erikson, one of the greatest writers on human development in the past century, saw the final stage of psychosocial development to be the development of wisdom and integrity, both of which arise from an acceptance of one's life, and its lessons learned.[14] Resilience is the ability to use this wisdom and apply life's lessons to adapt and accommodate to the challenges you are facing today.

Resilience is an active, ongoing process that can be developed and enhanced at any stage of life. It is not an innate quality that you have or do not have. As caregivers, you have a unique set of challenges and stressors that offer you a unique opportunity to grow. Resilience does not mean that you do not experience difficulty or distress. Resilience is not an ability to always react perfectly. Similar to taking on a new exercise program, resilience is a skill that can be learned, but it needs to be practiced in stressful situations. What caregivers need, then, is a set of tools with which to practice becoming more resilient in the face of difficulty and change. The following chapters will describe a sensible and positive set of core principles that, when practiced, can help you become more resilient, and improve the care you give to your loved one with dementia, enhancing the quality of life for both of you.

EXERCISE

Like the earlier example of Mike, you probably have instances from your own life where you faced difficult challenges but got through them with resilience. Remembering how we have successfully responded to crises in the past can inspire us in the present. Think of a time in your past life that was very stressful. Imagine yourself as you felt and thought about things at that time. On a separate sheet of paper, answer the following questions about that stressful period in your life. How did you get through that time? What kept you going? Who did you reach out to for support? What did you learn?

Now, think of your current life, focusing on what it is like to be providing care to someone you love who has dementia. Ask yourself the same questions as above, but reflecting on what is happening *now*. What are you doing to get through this time? What is keeping you going? Who are you reaching out to for support? What are you learning?

Compare your answers. What similarities and differences do you see in yourself between that time in the past and now? Are there strategies that you used to get through the difficult time in the past but are not using now? If other people helped you then, are there others who could help you now?

With these thoughts in mind, complete the Resilience Scale (Table 1).

TABLE 1. The Resilience Scale

Answer the following questions using a five-point rating scale. If you strongly disagree with a statement, circle "1." If you are neutral about the statement, circle "3." If you strongly agree with the statement, circle "5."

	Disagree				Agree
1. I usually manage one way or another.	1	2	3	4	5
2. Keeping interested in things is important to me.	1	2	3	4	5
3. I feel proud that I have accomplished things in my life.	1	2	3	4	5
4. I usually take things in stride.	1	2	3	4	5
5. I am friends with myself.	1	2	3	4	5
6. I feel I can handle many things at a time.	1	2	3	4	5
7. I am determined.	1	2	3	4	5
8. I can get through difficult times because I have experienced difficulty before.	1	2	3	4	5
9. Self-discipline is important.	1	2	3	4	5
10. I keep interested in things.	1	2	3	4	5
11. I can usually find something to laugh at.	1	2	3	4	5
12. My belief in myself gets me through hard times.	1	2	3	4	5
13. In an emergency, I am someone people can generally rely on.	1	2	3	4	5
14. I can usually look at a situation in a number of ways.	1	2	3	4	5
15. My life has meaning.	1	2	3	4	5
16. When I am in a difficult situation, I can usually find my way out of it.	1	2	3	4	5
17. I am resilient.	1	2	3	4	5

© The Resilience Scale, reprinted with permission (Young, 2001, pp. 155–157).

Now, look at the items where you rated yourself highly (score of 4 or 5). Think of these as your "resilient strengths," ways in which you already are dealing with your caregiver role, that are helping you. Now look at those items on which you gave yourself a low score (1 or 2). Think about what would have to change before you could give yourself a higher score. Is there anyone, or any change in your current routine and habits, that could help you? Think of *one* thing you could do differently as a caregiver in the next week that would build upon your past experiences and strengths. Try it, and see what happens.

Section II

THE PROGRAM:

Learning the Dementia Dance

Caring for a person with dementia will take you places you might not choose to go if you were in control. But since that is the reality of dementia care, you can learn to see some of its problems in new ways. Consider this story about an elderly, long-married couple.

Margie had not had a shower in two weeks. Her husband Bob was getting worried; his pretty wife, who had always been so meticulous about her appearance, was more and more often refusing to keep herself clean. Whenever he mentioned it was time to shower, she would say, "I already took a shower today," or, "I don't need one." Arguing and persuasion were useless. No matter what he said, no matter how many times he pointed out that she had not taken her shower and was beginning to smell bad, she would refuse. Yesterday, she had gotten angry and they had had a terrible fight that ended with Margie in tears and Bob storming out of the house for a walk around the block.

When he woke up this morning, Bob was determined not to lose his temper. He could see that it was useless; Margie immediately forgot their quarrels, but he felt bad for days afterward. As usual, Bob got up before Margie. He put on the morning coffee and headed to the bathroom to get cleaned up before she awoke. It was a chilly morning, so Bob turned on the bathroom heater, and while the shower water was warming up, grabbed a fluffy towel and robe, putting them within easy reach. He was still smarting from yesterday's fight with Margie, and, on an impulse, he stepped into their bedroom and looked at his sleeping wife of forty-two years. How much he loved her! As he bent down to kiss her, the clock radio turned on, set to their favorite station, an oldies station that played dance band music from the 1930s and 1940s. Margie opened her eyes and smiled sweetly, reaching up to Bob. He helped her up and they began to dance gently around the bedroom. Suddenly, Bob had an idea. As he and his wife danced, he began to shimmy her out of her nightgown. Girlish, she giggled but did not resist. As they danced, he led her toward the bathroom, which was now warm and steamy from the running shower. Once in the bathroom, he quickly stepped out of his own pajamas and danced her into the large step-in shower stall. Together, he and Margie shared a shower, the first she had taken without resistance in many, many months.

Many family caregivers will find elements of this story sadly familiar. For persons with progressive dementia, personal care is often an ongoing struggle. And not just personal care; as we discussed in the opening pages of this book, every aspect of daily life becomes a challenge. Persons with dementia forget how to feed and dress themselves, how to shave and shower, and how to do the simple and complex chores and daily activities that have been routine for decades. To further complicate matters, every person with dementia is unique. Some become violent and aggressive; others, happy and placid. One person seems oblivious to his memory and thinking problems, and easily gets angry and resentful at family attempts to offer assistance, while another recognizes early on that it is time to stop driving or move into assisted living. Most frustrating of all, dementia symptoms are a moving target. The mother who is happy and cooperative with one daughter can be hostile and resistant with another. The husband who has had a clear conversation with his wife about finances this morning may, in the accountant's office, deny ever agreeing to the plan. The wife who is looking forward to her only child getting married may refuse to leave the house on the wedding day, and attempts to change her mind eventually result in a catastrophic reaction, a complete emotional and behavioral meltdown.

So, what is a family member to do? Educational materials and self-help books about dementia provide many ideas for managing specific memory-related and behavior problems, but, inevitably, the problems that catch you by surprise are not discussed. In my years of experience working with hundreds of persons with dementia, and their families, I have become convinced that what caregivers need is a broad approach to dementia care, not a list of solutions to specific difficulties. Caregivers need a simple set of core principles to follow that will allow them to not only survive, but also thrive in an environment that is constantly changing and that often turns all their preconceived notions about themselves and their relationship with their loved one upside down.

I opened this section with the story about Bob and Margie for several reasons. First, the story offers us a fabulous example of resilient caregiving. Bob had tried all the usual, reasonable techniques to get Margie to take a shower. He had reminded her, reasoned with her, and scolded her, but nothing worked. He knew that taking a regular shower was important; it was not just something that could be ignored indefinitely. Bob had to find a way to get the job done, but there was no book or counselor in the world that would have suggested he dance Margie into the shower. In coming up with this solution, Bob demonstrated a number of characteristics of resilient responding we discussed in Chapter 1. His showering plan was creative, infused with not only love for his wife, but also a twinkle of humor mixed with a willingness to try something different, *anything* different, just to see what would happen. Although Bob seemingly stumbled upon the idea by accident, he knew Margie liked ballroom dancing—this ability to build on past pleasant activities is a hallmark of creative problem solving in caregiving. By showering with his wife, Bob removed a number of possible obstacles that may have been keeping Margie from doing it herself. Although she had not been able to tell Bob, maybe Margie had become afraid of the noisy water, or she was unsure what to do in the bathroom. Maybe she simply did not like being bossed around, but if Bob was going to shower too, well, that was another story. Bob might never know the true reason Margie was willing to shower that day, but it did not really matter. It taught him the value of keeping moving and trying new strategies in response to constantly changing circumstances. When the next problem with Margie came up, Bob felt more confident that he would eventually be able to figure out what to do as well.

A second reason for including the story of Bob and Margie is that dancing is a useful metaphor for caring for someone with dementia. Think about your own experiences dancing. When my husband and I first started learning to dance, it was very challenging. He was tall; I was short. We both wanted to lead. The music would start to play and we would take off in different directions, or find ourselves keeping time to a different beat (maybe not even the one that was playing!). I felt embarrassed that I could not remember the steps when other people made it look so easy. The instructor would tell me to just relax, to feel in my body where my husband was leading me, and trust that the rest would take care of itself. It was hard, though, to give up control, to let myself believe that I could gracefully move along beside him, when I never knew when he was going to turn or twirl me around or make a sudden maneuver to avoid running into a wall I had not seen coming. Although, over time, dancing together has gotten easier, I have never achieved the fluid ease of some of my friends, who seem almost able to read their partners' minds as they swirl and weave around the dance floor.

Living with someone who has dementia is like this. You find yourself being led places you do not want to go. I often tell caregivers that the person with dementia is leading in this dance, and if they do not want to get their toes stepped on, the caregivers need to learn to follow! However, if we do not know what is going to happen next, the last thing in the world most of us want to do is give up control of the situation. Perhaps when you look around, it seems other caregivers are having an easier time. You may feel like there is something wrong with you, or that your loved one is making the situation more difficult than it needs to be. No matter how hard you try, it seems as if the two of you are moving to a different beat. This can be particularly difficult for spouses who, for decades, have known each other so well that they can anticipate one another's every move. Now, all the rules are changed, the rhythm is unfamiliar, the dance steps have changed, and you are having a very hard time keeping up. This is not surprising. We are not born knowing how to do the dementia dance. The direct approach to getting things done that Americans love is tremendously ineffective with someone who has forgotten the rules and lost the ability to understand why we think our rules are so important anyway. Caregivers need to learn to follow, or, at the very least, to lead very gently and with the knowledge that at times, you will have to let go of your plans and expectations about where the dance should be heading.

Finally, D.A.N.C.E. is an acronym for the five core principles that re-silient caregivers have taught me over the years in my practice, and the acronym will provide a structure for the remainder of this book. These five principles are easy to understand and remember, and can be adapted to virtually every dementia-related problem and unique caregiving situation. These principles are not necessarily simple to implement. However, like dancing and exercise, with practice you will learn to use them more quickly, and become better at figuring out how to individualize their use to match your style and circumstances. The five principles are:

D–**D**on't argue

A–**A**ccept the disease

N–**N**urture your physical and emotional health

C–use **C**reative problem solving

E–**E**njoy the moment with your loved one

The story of Bob and Margie illustrates all of these principles. Bob's reasonable attempts to convince Margie to shower had not only failed, but they had also created tremendous frustration and upset for them both. In contrast, when Bob stopped approaching the problem with logical argu-ments, and instead found a solution that was creative, pleasurable, and grounded in the deep affection he felt for his wife, the bathing problem was solved and the stressful bickering about it stopped. When he described the scene afterward, Bob noted that he had recently begun to understand that Margie was not being resistant to showering just to make life difficult for him. If she was not engaging in self-care activities that had always been important to her, it must be that she was not *able* to do so, and it was up to Bob to find a way to help her that left her pride intact and did not unnecessarily treat her like an invalid. The fact that he *had* found a way in this instance made Bob feel proud and more self-assured that he could manage whatever else came up down the road.

Obviously, dancing to the shower will not work for everyone. I am convinced, however, that caregivers can develop the ability to come up with their own solutions to those infinitely varied and continually surprising situations they encounter. In doing so, dementia care can become perhaps not easy, but certainly less burdensome, and infused with greater purpose and satisfaction. As with all forms of dancing, learning the dementia D.A.N.C.E. takes time, practice, and a willingness to sometimes fall down. I continue to learn from, and be inspired by, the many persons with dementia and the family caregivers whom I meet. In the remainder of this book, I will try to share with you some of what I have learned, with the hope that you, too, will be inspired with a desire to learn to D.A.N.C.E.

Chapter 2

D: DON'T ARGUE! ◆

One of the first things we learn as human beings is to argue. Look at how many very young children know how to say "no!" Arguing is a highly adaptive communication skill. We learn from experience that arguing increases the likelihood that we will get our way. It stimulates intellectual reasoning on both sides. Arguing helps establish hierarchy and power differentials in relationships. It blows off steam and it shows we care about a belief or value. At some level, every person alive has learned to argue, in the sense that we all use verbal techniques to persuade and correct other people, particularly those with whom we have the most intimate relationships.

"Argue" means to reason or to try to make one understand; it does not necessarily imply contention. For example, arguments presented by a high school debate team may be spirited as well as educative and influential, but they are not verbal attacks on the opposition. Unfortunately, arguing is often paired with other forms of persuasion that tend to provoke strong defensive reactions, such as criticism, judgment, and labeling. Both types of arguing behavior can be seen in the example below.

Joseph was an eighty-three-year-old widower whose failing health and memory made it unsafe for him to live alone. Six months ago, Joseph had moved in with his adult daughter,

Sarah, and Sarah's husband and teenage son. The transition had not been an easy one for any of them. Joseph continued to ask when he would be able to return to his own little house. He would become very angry when Sarah would answer, "This is your home now, Dad!" Joseph did not like the hustle and bustle of the younger family's lifestyle. He did not like being told what to do. He especially did not like his grandson's attitude and appearance. Night after night at dinner, Joseph scolded Josh for his sullen expression, his baggy clothes, his too-long hair, his table manners, his disrespectful friends, and his failure to be of more help around the house. Josh's predictably angry responses would further provoke his grandfather, and usually would trigger an argument with one or both of his parents, who felt that Josh should be more patient with Joseph. The tension in the household had become constant and intolerable.

One night, after Joseph had retired to his bedroom, Sarah, her husband Richard, and Josh gathered around the dining-room table to talk about what to do. The various options were examined. Joseph could be placed in a nursing home. Either he or Josh could eat dinner at a different time from the rest of the family. Sarah had tried reasoning with Joseph, but he only repeated his endless list of complaints about Josh's failings. Then Richard came up with an idea. The family agreed upon a secret "code," a common phrase ("Was there any mail for me today?") that could be spoken by any of them when Joseph started criticizing Josh. The code was a signal to ignore whatever Joseph was saying, unless it was something neutral or positive. As they talked about how Joseph had changed since he had developed dementia, the family realized that he did not really understand the impact of his hurtful behavior and could not intentionally control it. This code was a way the family could work together to break the cycle of fighting. The first time they tried it, they noticed that Joseph's tirade seemed to fizzle out after a while. Sarah,

Richard, and Josh felt closer to one another and a little amused, coconspirators in their secret experiment. After a few weeks, most of the nightly quarrels had ended, and life started to settle back down into a manageable routine.

Joseph and Josh had fallen into a destructive pattern of arguing at the dinner table; neither the old man nor the teenager liked being criticized or told what to do, and both felt strongly that they were "right" and the other person had to change. In contrast, Sarah's arguments with her father were a type of logical discussion intended to help Joseph see the obvious (that he lived with Sarah now) and do the mature thing (stop haranguing Josh at dinner every night). Significantly, Sarah's loving, reasonable conversations with Joseph (she would not have called them arguments) were no more effective in resolving the situation than were the angry confrontations between Joseph and Josh. Things did not begin to improve until both Sarah and Josh gave up all forms of argument, whether negative or positive, and tried a strategy that did not rely on verbal persuasion to work. Why should this be necessary? To answer that question, we need to know how dementia changes the way a person communicates with the world around him.

COMMUNICATION CHANGES IN DEMENTIA

Alzheimer's disease and other forms of dementia produce changes in the brain that interfere with a person's ability to think, reason, and remember. Among the earliest clinical symptoms of dementia are language impairments that affect a person's ability to reason in verbal terms, to communicate what they are feeling and experiencing, and to understand fully what other people are saying or intending.[1] These changes often appear subtle to the outside observer, making it difficult to appreciate how pervasive and catastrophic they are for the affected individual.

At first, there is word-finding trouble, or "anomia." Persons with dementia frequently are not able to think of a word they want to use, or they make mistakes, replacing words with others that have a similar sound ("brook" instead of "book"). As time progresses, they may be able to describe the function of an object but not its name; for example, the woman looking at a picture of a fork says, "It's for eating," and mimes the action of picking up food with a fork but cannot think of the word "fork." Word-finding difficulties are common even in older adults without dementia, and so this symptom is easily overlooked or dismissed as a minor inconvenience. It can, however, have a surprisingly large impact on daily life. First, it is a source of frustration and embarrassment for the individual, who increasingly finds himself struggling in mid-conversation with family, friends, neighbors, or professionals (e.g., his doctor or attorney). People who are embarrassed are more likely to be defensive and irritable, trying to cover up a difficulty that is made worse by spouses or children who correct them in public, or make fun of their slips.

Furthermore, word-finding problems can be symptomatic of more serious but undiagnosed perceptual disturbances (a difficulty called "agnosia"). For example, the woman who says the word "ball" when shown a picture of an orange may actually be losing the ability to visually discriminate between categories of small, round objects or to recognize familiar persons or household items.[2] This, potentially, has significant safety implications for individuals who are at risk to misidentify and misuse common cleaning products, utensils, small appliances, motorized vehicles, or power tools. Here is an example of a woman with dementia who no longer recognized a familiar part of her own car.

Jim brought Agnes to my clinic for an unscheduled emergency visit. Agnes was Jim's elderly next-door neighbor. That morning, when Jim had headed out to get his morning paper, he heard Agnes yelling for help. He hurried over and found her in a panic, standing outside her car. When Jim asked what was the matter, Agnes said she was heading for morning church, and when she opened her car door, she found something strange inside. She did not know what it was or how it got there, and she was afraid. Jim looked inside at the object Agnes was pointing to. It was the car's emergency brake.

Dementia-related changes in language also affect reading comprehension. There are many documented cases where a person with dementia is able to read aloud words that they no longer understand. As with object naming, even in its milder forms, this hidden decline can have a significant impact on a person's daily life and can lead to conflicts with those around them. People who are losing the ability to understand what they read are more likely to get lost because they cannot follow street signs or directions, but they may still insist that they are able to drive across town by themselves. Lifelong avid readers who are bored and restless, unable to follow a newspaper storyline or pick up a favorite book to read, may put unexplained demands on their loved ones to help them pass the time in other ways. Persons with dementia who are still working or doing volunteer work may begin to make mistakes and become very anxious about their ability to grasp on-the-job information that was once second nature but now has become too complicated. When challenged by coworkers or employers, they become defensive and angry.

In some cases, declining language function is manifested as difficulty with logical reasoning and judgment that is not obvious to the casual observer. Many persons with dementia retain the ability to make social chitchat about the weather, their daily activities, or the family, but cannot answer a direct question. When asked about a morning headline, the once-avid newspaper reader says, "Everything in the news is just the same! It's all so slanted I just don't pay attention anymore." When asked what she is fixing for Sunday dinner, the matriarch of a large family gazes at her cookbook and says, "Oh, we will all get together. We always do. We haven't decided yet what the plan is, but I'm sure it'll all work out all right."

This ability to talk easily and sociably can hide the fact that the person has become quite impaired and really does not know what he or she is talking about. Sadly, in extreme cases, family and friends only discover the elder's vulnerability when he or she is taken advantage of by some unscrupulous individual, as in this story:

Mary Ellen, a mortgage closing agent, was unsure what to do. The elderly man sitting in front of her said he wanted to sell his house to his middle-aged woman companion. All the paperwork seemed to be in order. The appraisal had been done, the finance fees were paid, and all that was left was this final series of signatures by both parties. But something just did not seem right. The seller was a jovial man who listened while Mary Ellen reviewed the terms of the sale, and then started to tell her a humorous story about his years as a pilot in World War II. When Mary Ellen tried to make sure the man understood that he was selling the house for well under current market value, the companion became impatient and tried to hurry the process along. When it was time to sign, the man became confused about what he was doing, even though Mary Ellen had just finished explaining the form. She asked the man if he had any adult children in the area who she could check with about a small detail in the application. When a daughter was contacted, she was horrified to learn that her father was about to sell his home to the woman who had recently moved in next door. None of his family knew anything about the proposed sale, or about the potential buyer.

Mary Ellen was the last in a line of finance professionals who had talked with the pleasant elderly man about selling his house and failed to detect that he was not actually able to understand the arrangements that he was agreeing to, or to think through the consequences of his actions. If it had not been for Mary Ellen's willingness to trust her intuition and take time in the midst of her busy day to check into things a little more closely, the man would have been swindled out of his home.

In most cases, of course, the consequences are much less dire. The more common scenario is that although we know our loved ones have dementia, we still get fooled by the fact that they look fine from the outside and can put sentences together that make sense in a given conversation. We thus expect that mom will behave in rational, predictable ways, and we become frustrated and upset when that does not happen.

One caregiver told me that her elderly tenant, who had Alzheimer's disease, had for many years helped fold the laundry and clean the kitchen as part of her contribution to the group home where she lived. The tenant had recently stopped doing her chores, and even if she could be talked into starting one, she would lose interest after a few minutes and leave her job unfinished. The caregiver, who had become accustomed to the extra help that she badly needed, resented her tenant's change in habits. She knew the tenant had a diagnosis of dementia, but since the tenant otherwise remained very outspoken and independent in her self-care activities, her "unwillingness to lend a hand" around the house appeared to be intentional.

Because her tenant did not "look" demented—she could still manage her daily affairs without help, and was very assertive in her opinions—the caregiver felt that the tenant was being thoughtless and lazy. It is at such moments that we are likely to fall into an argument. What can be done instead?

CHANGING OLD COMMUNICATION PATTERNS IS HARD

Before we talk about what we can do differently with our loved ones who have dementia, let us think about what happens when we disagree with *anyone*—our spouse, our children, our coworkers, or our friends. One of the first things you may notice is how fast anger happens. When someone says or does something that I strongly disagree with or do not like, I have an immediate visceral response. I can feel a reaction in my body that is much like fear—my stomach churns, and I start to feel shaky and tense. I become poised to react, to convince the other person to do what is "right," or to see things my way. Depending on the circumstance, I may make a matter-of-fact statement of disagreement or disapproval. I may offer a criticism or "correction" of the other person's behavior or perspective. Sometimes, I keep my disapproval to myself, but it slips out in other ways—a raised eyebrow, a scowling expression, a sharp retort, or a sarcastic comment. I may start rushing around, slamming papers down a little too hard, or driving a little too fast. Whatever my external response, underneath, I usually feel my anger is justified. Even without raising my voice, I make my displeasure clear.

In my better moments, I am able to slow myself down, take a deep breath, and find a reasonable tone in which to present my points of view carefully. I try not to blame the other person. I may even be aware of their side of the situation and try to find an acceptable compromise. Although most people would not consider this kind of response to be "arguing," the underlying goal is the same—I want control. I want someone or something in the world to be different than it is. Furthermore, even when I am willing to change and compromise, I want the other person to make some changes, too. The most challenging situations are those where the other person is unable or uninterested in seeing or doing things my way. Learning to "accept the things I cannot change" with humor and grace, and being able to distinguish these from situations where I can make a difference, are sometimes very difficult.[3]

Every one of us has people and situations in our lives that trigger impatience, anger, resentment, or feelings of entitlement, but persons with dementia and their family caregivers have more than their daily share. Persons with dementia lose their ability to take a deep breath and modulate their responses. An underlying flash of temper or fear is more likely to come out at unpredictable moments and in unexpected ways. They are more likely to behave in ways that are unsafe, to neglect personal duties or self-care needs, and to act in socially inappropriate ways. They can no longer handle responsibilities that they have managed successfully in the past, but they often still *think* that they can. Thus, there are many opportunities in the course of a day for caregivers to try and persuade their loved ones to behave differently.

Unfortunately, arguing, even in its most reasonable and rational forms, is spectacularly ineffective with persons who have dementia. It is not just because their ability to think things through, to reason verbally, and to comprehend spoken logic is deteriorating. The problem is compounded by the fact that as logical, verbal communication breaks down, persons with dementia become keenly sensitive to nonverbal communication cues such as the caregiver's tone of voice, body posture, and facial expressions. The words you say may be calm and reasonable, but if your underlying mood is critical irritability or resentment, chances are that mood is what the demented individual will respond to, not the words. To make matters even worse, the dementing illness interferes with one's ability to modulate emotional responding, leading to what has been called "catastrophic reactions." Suddenly, the person with dementia becomes unreasonably agitated, upset, or even aggressive in response to a minor frustration or caregiver request. Faced with such an extreme and unprovoked outburst from their loved ones, caregivers find it very difficult to stay calm and pleasant. The temptation to snap back or fall into argument is very strong. The following example illustrates how one caregiver broke this vicious cycle.

Mark was a big man, whose arthritis and chronic back problems made it difficult for him to move around. He also had Alzheimer's disease, which had made him uncharacteristically surly and irritable. The worst time was in the morning, when his tiny wife, Sally, had to help him get out of bed. As she lifted and coaxed and prompted, Mark would become more and more impatient. The scene inevitably culminated with Mark sitting up in a wheelchair screaming at Sally, who was either yelling back or reduced to tears. It was exhausting.

One morning, Sally was determined to try and avoid an argument. When Mark grumbled about having to sit up in bed, she responded by commenting what a beautiful morning it was. When he snapped at her for hurting his back as she changed his clothes, she calmly apologized, saying she would try to be more careful next time. When she finally was able to get Mark transferred over to the chair beside the bed, she gave him a hug and said, "Honey, you did a great job getting up this morning."

To Sally's astonishment, Mark grumbled some response but he did not yell at her, and instead, immediately became distracted by something outside the window. Talking later to a visiting home health nurse, Sally explained what happened. "It was like a lightning bolt hit me! I realized that what was triggering Mark's morning screaming episodes was the way I was acting while I helped get him out of bed. Usually by the time I finally got Mark up, I was feeling so unappreciated and fed up that I would give a big sigh of relief, and collapse. When I changed my tone and approach—when I stopped sighing and rolling my eyes and instead thanked Mark for doing the best he could—the mornings began to go much better!"

"DON'T JUST DO SOMETHING, STAND THERE!"

At the start of the scenario described above, Sally was having a hard time tolerating Mark's physical needs and continual complaints.[4] If you look up the word "tolerance" in the dictionary, most of the definitions are about "gritting it out." However, one definition has to do with the optimal space between two objects. If you have a machine, like a watch or a part in your car, and the moving parts are too close together, they do not work properly. They get ratcheted down or rub against each other and cause friction. There is low tolerance here. On the other hand, if they are too far apart, they rattle around. They have to be in just the right operating distance from one another. Similarly, effective communication between any two people in a relationship needs to have the right balance between closeness or moving in, and distance or giving the other space. It is often counterintuitive—when you are frightened or angry, you tend to move in and defend yourself, attack, or try to solve the problem, when in fact that may be the very time you need to stop, take a deep breath, and retreat from the battle.[5]

At some level, most caregivers have figured out that trying to reason or argue with a person who has dementia is a futile task. What alternatives are there, however, when your loved one is doing something that threatens his or her health, safety, or well-being, or, more commonly, is simply driving you crazy? The right alternative may be to try something totally new, and that something new is most often a variant of doing (or saying) *nothing*—at least nothing that you would normally do or say in this situation. This can be

incredibly difficult. We talked earlier about how quickly angry and frightened responses show up, and how easily they are entwined with feelings of
stubbornness and old resentments. This is true for persons with dementia as
well as caregivers, but only you, the caregiver, can change to make things
better. You have to learn how to catch yourself in that split second before
you react with criticism, correction, explanations, impatience, or even reasonable discussion about an important topic. In that moment, you can ask
yourself, "Is what I'm about to do or say going to help this situation?" If it
has not helped the last five times you have done it—or if it helps occasionally
but most of the time makes things worse—you need to figure out something
else to try. Sometimes, presenting the person who has dementia with a
seemingly different request accomplishes the goal.

> Clark's driving had become very bad. Everyone in the family
> had begged him to stop, but he refused to give up his license
> or let anyone else drive his manual transmission car. Clark's
> brother and primary caregiver, Paul, lived next door. One
> morning over coffee, Paul told Clark that he had gone to
> the doctor, and the doctor had told Paul that he needed to
> exercise his arms more. In fact, a manual transmission car
> was just what he needed! Could he, Paul, borrow Clark's car
> for a little while? To help his brother out, Clark reluctantly
> "loaned" his car to Paul, and even let Paul drive Clark around
> to his appointments to "get more exercise." Clark occasion-
> ally asked how Paul's arms were doing, but soon forgot about
> driving the car that now sat in his brother's garage.

In the story above, Paul decided to stop arguing with Clark about his
driving. He made a deliberate and conscious decision to not do what was
familiar and automatic every time he saw his brother climb into his car. But
if he was not going to argue, how *was* he going to help keep his brother
safe? In this case, Paul deflected his arguments and appealed to his brother's
lifelong willingness to help people in need. By "doing nothing" directly
about stopping Clark's driving, Paul managed to gently wean his brother
from using the car, and the problem was solved.

You can see that "doing nothing" in the midst of dementia care is a very sophisticated skill. It is analogous to the incredible coordination and discipline that you see in ballroom dancing competitions. Each person in the couple must know when to lean into their partner, and also when to step aside and get out of the way. There is an art to knowing when to hold back. It requires thinking beyond the immediate moment to a future point, and seeing the best way to get there, which is often a route you have never taken before.

ALTERNATIVES TO ARGUING: SOME COMMUNICATION TOOLS TO TRY

It takes practice to see the big picture and recognize when something you are doing is not working and a new plan is needed.[6] Arguing does not work. Even when you know you are right, and do not believe you should have to change, you need to give it up. In the long run, it will make your life easier. We will talk elsewhere in this book about how one can come up with creative solutions to difficult problems. It is important to note, however, that effective communication—that is, relating to your loved one without arguing, reasoning, or debating—is the foundation for all problem-solving strategies in dementia care. No matter how good your ideas are, if you have not given up arguing, you will continue to get stuck. There are several principles underlying effective communication that are particularly useful for caregivers who want to stop arguing but just do not know how. Give them a try! No matter how awkward they feel in the beginning, with time and practice these strategies become automatic and will greatly enrich your relationship with your loved one who has dementia.

Tool #1: Caring Detachment

The first secret to being able to give up arguing is detachment. Detachment is not emotional indifference or pretense that nothing is the matter when, in fact, you are seething or frantically worried inside. Rather, it is a very loving action of genuinely accepting the other person as he is, not as you want him to be. Detachment is the ability to step back and see the forest, not just the trees. It is the ability to respond to the person's dementia that is causing the problem, not the person himself. If you can appreciate the reality that your loved one has a brain disease that is affecting his or her ability to think, react, and understand the world as you do, you will be halfway to taking your loved one's behavior less personally, and being better able to respond in new, more effective, ways.

It is possible to be detached in a caring and therapeutic way only if you are really listening to the other person. Dr. Linda Teri, an internationally renowned geriatric psychologist, has coined the jingle "Listen with respect; comfort and redirect" as a way of helping caregivers think about effective communication.[7] Listening with respect means keeping quiet, withholding your own reactions, long enough for the other person to feel heard. It means trying to hear what the person is really feeling underneath what he is saying. When a person with dementia has an angry outburst over being asked to take medication, you may find it helpful to put yourself in his shoes. How might he or she be feeling right now? Perhaps he is tired of always being told what to do, or annoyed at the tone of voice or the way you asked. Maybe she is fearful because she does not really understand what the medications are for, or is mad at being interrupted from a nap. If you can figure out what underlies your loved one's words and actions, and can respond to those feelings with comfort and reassurance instead of taking personally what was said, that is caring detachment at its best.

I have a therapist friend who says, "He who cares the least has the most power."[8] People who are very much caught up in their feelings and reactions often have less power to be effective. It is noteworthy that in the opening story in this chapter, the least emotionally involved family member (Richard) was the one who was able to come up with a solution that helped break the destructive nightly arguments between Joseph and his grandson Josh. Richard was the only one who was able to step back and look at the situation with a fresh perspective. Like Joseph's family and Clark's brother, you are going to have to rely increasingly on ways of communication with your loved one that do not require reasonable discussion or persuasion.

There are some things that you will just need to stop asking or telling your loved one; some decisions that he or she can no longer help you make. This is a very painful realization not only for spouses, who are accustomed to sharing every important life event and decision, but also for adult children, siblings, or other relatives and friends who must accept that a much-admired and competent individual is no longer able to take charge of his or her own life. Family caregivers sometimes feel that they are being dishonest or disrespectful by censoring what they say to their loved ones. An alternative viewpoint is that you are graciously accommodating your loved one's very real limitations, regardless of whether he or she is aware of them. You are being polite.

Tool #2: Be Polite or Even P.O.L.I.T.E.

The second communication principle is based on the fact that how you talk to someone with dementia can always make your situation better or worse. That is true, of course, in any human interaction, but in the world of caregiving it needs to be more deliberately considered than you may be accustomed to. Your spoken words, your tone of voice, your body language, and your judicious use of humor can all impact how smoothly your day goes. In the previous story, Sally stopped rolling her eyes, scolding, and hurrying, and wound up treating Mark with greater love and respect. She did not really know what specific trigger for Mark's outbursts had been eliminated, but she did know that things were much easier in the morning after she changed her approach.

It sounds simplistic, but simple kindness and courtesy go a long way toward making things right with someone who has dementia. You know how you want to be treated. When you greet people, you want them to smile back. You want to be taken seriously. You want to feel that you are respected and liked. Imagine what it can be like to have a dementing illness. You are continually being told you are wrong and that you cannot do things you want to do. Even your efforts to help out are frequently rebuffed. You feel useless. As caregivers, we need to resist the temptation to treat persons with dementia as "drunken toddlers" who have lost all sense of self and are fumbling around inadvertently, destroying whatever comes in their path. Older adults with dementia are the spouses, parents, siblings, friends, and community and business leaders who have helped build the world we live in. Remembering the respect, gratitude, and care that we owe these individuals can provide the motivation we need to be gracious when we offer our care and support. In Table 2, the word "polite" is broken out as an acronym to help you remember a collection of specific courteous communication skills that will enhance your ability to avoid arguments with your loved one.

Tool #3: Distraction

The third and final key communication strategy is distraction. Redirecting an agitated, upset, or perseverative individual with dementia away from whatever has gotten him stuck is a powerful tool for avoiding and getting out of arguments that are brewing. In the situation below, a resilient caregiver accidentally discovered the power of distraction.

At about five each evening, Amy wanted to go home. She *was* home, of course, but for some reason, at that time of day she seemed to not recognize her husband, Arthur, or the house in which they had raised their three children. If allowed, she would walk out the front door and head down the street, and getting her turned around and back inside was not easy. Arthur tried bolting the door, but his wife's inability to get it open made her even more upset. One night, while Arthur was trying to convince his wife to calm down, the telephone rang. It was Elsa, their youngest daughter. Arthur asked Elsa to talk to her mother. In a few minutes, Amy was content, listening to news about the grandkids. At Arthur's request, the three kids set up a nightly phone tree, alternating calls to their mom, right before dinnertime. While Amy talked on the phone, Arthur would finish preparing dinner. With this soothing change in their nightly routine, Amy's requests to go home greatly diminished.

TABLE 2. P.O.L.I.T.E. Tools for Effective Communication in Persons with Dementia

Patience	Don't be in a hurry.
	Ask or say one thing at a time.
	Allow a moment of time before repeating instructions.
	Speak slowly and clearly—not necessarily louder!
Organize and observe	Break tasks into simple steps.
	Use hand gestures to demonstrate what you are asking the person to do (pick up glass and drink, etc.)
	Written signs and notes are helpful in the early stages of memory loss.
	Think of the person's behavior as a cue to how he or she is feeling right now.
Laughter	Smile!
	Use a warm, friendly, and respectful tone of voice.
	Cheerfulness and gentle humor can help in difficult moments.
	Give sincere praise for even a simple job done well.
Ignore what you can	"Pick your battles": Refrain from correcting the other person unless what he is saying or doing is unsafe or unhealthy.
Tone of voice	Avoid giving orders or acting "bossy."
	Use pleasant, matter-of-fact statements (e.g., "I have your three o'clock medications") instead of commands.
	Ask yourself: Would I want the other person to be talking to me this way? Persons with dementia become very sensitive to nonverbal cues such as tone of voice, facial expression, body gestures, and mood. If you are angry or upset, they are more likely to act the same.
Eye and body contact	Look directly at the other person when speaking or listening. You want to be sure you have his attention.
	Stand or sit at eye level. This helps if the person is hard of hearing, and keeps him or her from feeling as if you are talking down to them.
	Gentle touch can help orient the person to you, as well as provide comfort and reassurance.

There are several ways to distract someone. As in this case with Amy, the first distraction tool involves helping the person with dementia do something that is pleasant and enjoyable so as to redirect her away from whatever is upsetting. Playing familiar music or a favorite video, asking the loved one to help with simple chores like sorting clothes, looking at old photo albums and family letters, and taking time out to have a snack or get a back rub are all pleasant distractions. Amy's children calling at the time of day when she was most likely to become anxious about wanting to go home was an excellent example of how distraction can be used to help someone with dementia. It also helped Arthur, who was now able to do his nightly dinner preparation without having to stop and try to calm his wife. Finally, the nightly calls had the added advantage of helping Arthur and Amy's busy children grow a little closer to their mom. In the big picture, everyone benefited from this solution.

Distraction also requires some selective ignoring, since helping the person with dementia focus on something pleasant often involves not attending to what he or she is saying or doing at the moment. The earlier story of Sally and Mark's morning routine was a good example of this strategy. Sally distracted Mark by first ignoring his complaints and then changing the subject to something more pleasant and neutral like the beautiful weather outside. This communication tool can seem very awkward when you first try it out; it seems rude to ignore something that is said directly to you, and then to respond back with a totally unrelated comment. I often tell caregivers that having dementia is like driving a car on a muddy road. It is easy to have your wheels lose traction in the muddy ruts and not be able to turn off the road without help. When caregivers help their loved ones get some traction, to turn away from depressive or anxious vocalizations, restless agitation, or some dangerous activity by ignoring and distracting, it is not rude. It is providing very, very good care.

Another variant of distraction and selective ignoring that helps avoid arguments involves waiting until later to ask persons with dementia to do something that they do not want to do. It is the rare request that, in reality, must be handled this very minute. Your loved one's forgetfulness at times like this is an ally. She may refuse her medication now, but take it happily in fifteen minutes when you come back and offer it to her another way.

Whatever is causing conflict between the two of you often disappears if you can give the person with dementia a little time to stop thinking about it, and give yourself a few minutes to come up with another approach. For example,

> Julie, our research interviewer, was out doing a home visit. One of her tasks was to retrieve a wristband that a subject with dementia had been wearing for the past week to monitor her nighttime sleep and activity. When Julie went to take it off, the subject recoiled, saying, "No! You can't have that, it's my watch!" Julie said, "Oh, OK," and went about conducting the rest of her interview with the subject and the home caregiver. When she was ready to leave, she turned back to the subject, sat down beside her, and pointed to her wrist saying, "It looks like this watch is broken. We need to take it in to be repaired. Is it all right with you if I take it off?" The subject readily agreed.

Alternatively, in other situations, asking someone else to give you a hand is the best solution. Whatever the reason, it is not unusual for persons with dementia to object very strongly to receiving certain kinds of help from one person, but to accept it calmly from another. In such cases, the path of least resistance can be to take advantage of this gift, rather than insisting that you must figure out how to make the situation work by yourself. Assistance with activities of daily living—showering, toileting, medication management, dressing—can make those tasks go more smoothly when the best "assistant" can be found.

> Mr. M would not take a shower. His frail and elderly wife was at her wit's end wondering what to do. In desperation, one of their daughters contacted a local home health service and arranged for an aide to come and shower her father once a week. The first day a young, attractive female aide came and Mr. M's wife was sure her husband would refuse to cooperate with the shower. However, the aide was professional and authoritative. When she announced, "Mr. M, it's time for me

to help you with your shower," he immediately went off with her without complaint. Mr. M's wife was a little annoyed, but also bemused and grateful that her husband would acquiesce so readily to a stranger, when he was so stubborn with her and their children.[9]

Finally, sometimes the very best way to distract someone from unsafe or problematic activities is to remove whatever has got his attention. In the chapters to come, we will talk at length about removing the "triggers" for problematic behaviors, but it is worth touching on briefly here. In cases where something in the environment is causing arguments, getting it out of sight—as in the case with Clark's car and the example below—may be just what is needed to help the demented individual forget and move on.

Bill wanted to paint the fence outside. Unfortunately, the fence was on the neighbors' property and the neighbors did not want the fence painted. His wife discovered that when she removed all the paint cans from the garage, and the paint brushes that still hung over Bill's work bench, he stopped talking about painting the fence.

SUMMARY

Changes occur in the brain as a result of Alzheimer's disease and other dementias, which affect one's ability to think and comprehend written and verbal information. These changes in verbal communication affect the way a person reasons with, and responds to, the world around him. Externally, however, these changes may not be apparent. This leaves friends and family members of persons with dementia in a difficult position. If the demented individuals seem still verbally intact, their caregivers may be prone to overestimate their abilities and become impatient with their failures to respond to verbal explanations and reasoning. If a person is clearly very confused, the caregiver might assume that he does not understand when he is being talked about in public or when the caregiver is upset and irritated with his or her job. Both assumptions can contribute to conflicts between the person with dementia and the caregiver, as well as to an exacerbation of dementia-related behavioral disturbances. Because it is so difficult to really know what the person with dementia is capable of at any point in time, and how best to respond, the best solution is for the caregiver to adopt a strategy of using effective communication that is based on (1) caring detachment, (2) being polite and using P.O.L.I.T.E. communication skills, and (3) using distraction to help move on when difficult moments arise. Remember, good communication is the foundation of good dementia care.

◆ EXERCISE

One of the most difficult steps to effective communication with persons who have dementia is "listening with respect." We are so quick to leap to judgment about why people do the things they do, that we often forget there may be alternative explanations that can be more helpful in figuring out what to do in a situation. This exercise is an attempt to help you see that the assumptions we make about people's behavior influence how we respond. If you can practice caring detachment and change your under-lying assumptions (or at least consider other possibilities), it will be easier to stop arguing and generate alternative strategies to try.

Instructions

Read the scenario below. Pretend you are the adult child caregiver who has gotten out of bed to come help your dad, only to be yelled at. Imagine how you might feel at that moment. Then circle five adjectives from the first box that could describe your demented father. (In a real situation, you might not choose any of the adjectives in the box; for this exercise, however, pick five.)

You are an only child caregiver for your father, a wealthy business executive with mild dementia. You are concerned that he is no longer able to live alone, and you tell him you think he should consider moving to an assisted-living setting. He gets very angry, and accuses you of just wanting to steal his money. He says that he has the right to live however he wants, and it is none of your business. Late that night, he calls saying he cannot find his wallet and he thinks he has been robbed. He wants you to come right over to help him look for it. When you arrive at his house, he is asleep in his favorite chair. He snaps at you when you wake him up, and demands to know why you are here so late.

Arrogant	Lazy	Manipulative	Righteous
Selfish	Domineering	Untrusting	Weak
Thoughtless	Proud	Deceitful	Ungrateful
Willful	Incompetent	Untrustworthy	Self-centered
Stubborn	Abusive	Demanding	Irresponsible
Does not listen	Indifferent	Confused	Disrespectful
Paranoid	Controlling	Opinionated	Critical

If you, as caregiver, saw your father's behavior in terms of these five adjectives, what are you likely to do or say?

_____

_____

Now reread the story, but this time, circle five characteristics to describe your father only from this second box of adjectives.

Frightened	Successful	Forgetful	Embarrassed
Worried	Independent	Assertive	Confused
Defensive	Smart	Responsible	Needy
Nervous	Good	Bereaved	Indecisive
Sad	Thoughtful	Competent	Strong
Anxious	Funny	Self-made	Cautious
Self-deprecating	Proud	Insecure	Lost

Given the way you have now described your father, what are some things you might do or say?

_____

_____

Did seeing your father and his behavior in different terms change your response? Can you think of any situations in your own life where changing your interpretation of the behavior of a person with dementia would have helped you avoid an argument?

_____

_____

Chapter 3

A: ACCEPT THE DISEASE ◆

Inability to accept the reality of dementia is one thing that can undermine your best attempts to avoid arguments and communicate effectively. Resilient caregivers are those who deeply understand how dementia impacts the person they are caring for, and, as a result, can adopt realistic expectations for their loved one and for themselves. Unfortunately, sometimes it takes a shock for us to appreciate exactly what is going on.

John and Mary were traveling through Canada. While browsing the shops on the street outside their hotel one chilly afternoon, Mary indicated she wanted to run up to the room to grab her sweater. Some hours later, after searching everywhere for her on his own, John notified the city authorities. Soon, it was discovered that John and Mary's car was missing from the lot where it had been parked. Frantic, John waited for news about his wife. After two days, their daughter called from their hometown, several hundred miles away, to say that Mary had arrived safe and sound. The daughter noted that Mary was "spitting mad" when she drove up to a neighbor's house, wanting to know "where the heck did John go?"

John had been having trouble believing that his lovely, capable wife really had Alzheimer's disease. The doctors said her memory was bad, but hey, so was his. Isn't that normal for old folks like us? The Canada trip was a wake-up call. For most caregivers, the point at which they make contact with the reality of a dementia diagnosis is not as spectacular as in John and Mary's case. However, for every resilient caregiver, there comes a point at which he must accept that his loved one has a brain disease, and that the expectations he had for this individual no longer apply. Over time, the person with dementia cannot continue to prepare nightly meals, organize the taxes, or be a volunteer bookkeeper at the neighborhood co-op. Failure to accept the reality of their loved ones' limitations can lead caregivers to neglect safety issues and reject available community services. Caregivers who minimize the severity of their loved ones' cognitive impairments are also more likely to take personal offense at problematic behavior, whether it is some embarrassing public faux pas or refusal to take part in chores and activities that have always been his or her responsibility in the past.

In this chapter, we will discuss how resilient caregivers can help themselves and their loved ones maintain a good quality of life by finding new ways to accept their situation. Three aspects of acceptance will be considered. The first has to do with accepting the dementia diagnosis. Given the variability and inconsistency of symptoms during the early stages of the disease, it is not surprising that caregivers often have difficulty accepting a family member's dementia diagnosis. Caregivers also, sometimes, struggle with acceptance because of what the words "Alzheimer's disease" and "dementia" represent for them and their loved one. Many people see the dementia diagnosis as a death sentence and an end to the quality of life that they have heretofore enjoyed. American culture places a high value on autonomy, self-determination, and achievement. The gradual constricting of personal freedom and increasing interdependence experienced by persons with dementia and their family caregivers is a terrifying prospect; it can be alleviated by finding purpose and opportunity for growth in the experience.

A second, related aspect of acceptance is that caregivers need to accept the real limitations that they and their loved ones must now live with. As we saw in Chapter 2 on communication, many problems that a dementia sufferer experiences are invisible to the observer's eye. As a consequence, it is very easy to assume that the person you are caring for is still able to continue participating in activities that he or she has done for years. Once you really accept his or her dementia diagnosis, however, you may discover that some of what you are expecting or asking of your loved one is no longer realistic—or at least, it will not be in the foreseeable future. You will have to start doing some things differently. Accepting the new limits also means having realistic expectations for *yourself* and for those who could be of help to you. No matter how skillful a multitasker you have been in the past, now it is time to ask yourself whether carrying it all alone is necessary or reasonable. You will need to look around and realistically evaluate your support systems. Probably, there are people in your life who could make your life easier if you would only ask; and there may be others who you feel should be there to give a hand, but whose involvement would be more of a burden than a help. We will talk at length in Chapter 4 about the actual process of rallying your support systems in order to nurture yourself. In this chapter, however, we will consider what, if any, unrealistic expectations you may currently have about your and your loved one's roles and abilities, and what changes might be made to simplify your lifestyle or routines.

The third, critical aspect of acceptance for resilient caregivers is learning to accept your thoughts, feelings, memories, and reactions; in other words, learning to truly accept and love yourself and your situation as it really is, not as you would like it to be. It is very painful to see someone you care about being unable to do things that came easily to them in the past. Caregivers often feel that if they accept the fact that their loved ones have a progressive neurological disease that has no cure, they are "giving up" and abandoning the persons with dementia. They want their loved ones to keep fighting and trying to stave off the inevitable decline. They feel angry when that does not happen, and then guilty for getting angry with someone who is not responsible for his or her behavior. Adult children find themselves torn between the needs of a parent and those of their own spouse and children. Parents feel reluctant to burden their adult children with their needs, but sometimes also feel resentful that these same children are not doing more for their demented mother or father. Spouses are ashamed when they find themselves feeling bitter over the loss of lifelong retirement dreams, or when they catch themselves wishing that the loved one would die rather than continue to live a life that no longer seems worthwhile.

True self-acceptance is the most challenging, the most ongoing, and, perhaps, the most important of the acceptance domains that we will be discussing. We will talk about ongoing empirical research that is examining psychological acceptance, and strategies for helping you make room for the full orchestra of inner experiences that accompany the caregiver role. As you begin to practice all three forms of acceptance, it will be increasingly possible to take the remaining steps of the dementia D.A.N.C.E.—nurturing yourself and your loved one, creatively solving whatever problems come your way, and enjoying each moment as it comes.

ACCEPTING THE DIAGNOSIS

Clinicians rely on a variety of tools to diagnose dementia in persons experiencing progressive changes in their memory and thinking. First and foremost is the clinical interview. Persons experiencing the early signs of dementia often initially consult their physicians for reasons that are unrelated to their cognitive difficulties. Studies have shown that in the two years preceding a dementia diagnosis, there is frequently an increase in the number of scheduled medical appointments, which drop off once the diagnosis is made.[1] A physician or nurse may recognize something is "not right" in this escalating pattern of visits, and pursue a dementia diagnosis on his or her own. Alternatively, sometimes, patients come in asking for help, wondering whether their increasing memory problems are normal for their age or something more serious. The most common scenario, however, is that a concerned family member notices his or her loved one is having difficulty at home and either contacts a health-care professional directly or urges that person to go in for an evaluation.

In the ideal situation, the health-care provider who conducts the initial evaluation interview will meet separately with both the person with dementia and one or more involved family members. This allows family members to reveal their honest concerns about how their relative is functioning in his or her everyday activities and relationships, and gives the provider a chance to get a good history of the onset and duration of the presenting problems. This process also helps the provider determine if there are differences in opinion between the person with suspected dementia, and his or her family and friends about what is going on, or if there are unique social or environmental circumstances that will become important to deal with if a dementia diagnosis is made. The private interview with the person who has dementia will include a brief cognitive screening test and a physical examination. The physical exam usually includes a neurological screening and a limited number of laboratory tests to rule out common, treatable causes of cognitive decline in older adults, including use of certain medications.[2] Specialists such as geriatric psychiatrists or social workers may be consulted as part of the evaluation and treatment process. For physicians experienced with dementia assessments, the diagnostic accuracy for dementia when these procedures are followed is quite high.

So why is it that, even after these routine procedures have been completed, some family members still do not believe their loved one has dementia? Let us look at one common scenario where that has occurred.

Sophie brought her father, Mike, to the geriatric clinic to be evaluated for changes in his behavior. Mike just had not seemed himself since Sophie's mom died last year. He had become careless in keeping up the house; and when Sophie was helping tidy up one day, she noticed several overdue bill notices and several checks missing out of his checkbook that had not been entered into the register. A lifelong Catholic, he no longer went to Sunday Mass. Sophie's sister, Ann, who lived out of town, attributed these changes to depression over their mother's death, even though Mike's symptoms had not improved after several months of taking an antidepressant medication. Although he was a college graduate, Mike had difficulty answering when the doctor asked him to do simple subtractions or remember important family facts like how many children he had. When Mike was eventually given a diagnosis of early dementia during a family conference with the doctor, Ann became very angry. "You don't know what you're talking about!" Ann shouted at the doctor and then stormed out of the room.

It is easy to see why Ann had a hard time accepting the fact that her father had dementia. First, it seemed that all of Mike's problems started after his wife had died. It was only logical that he would be depressed after that and less attentive to details like paying his bills, or less interested in doing things with other people. The fact that Mike had not responded to treatment for his depression was not impressive to Ann, who herself still greatly missed her mother and was skeptical that a medication could really help her dad get over her mother's death. Second, Ann did not live close to her father. She did not see many of the subtle, day-to-day changes that concerned Sophie, who was around Mike on a much more regular basis. In fact, when Ann came into town for the family meeting, Mike had seemed like his old self. They had spent an evening looking at family photos, laughing over stories from the days when Ann and Sophie had been kids. It was hard for Ann to believe that her father, who seemed so vibrant during her brief visit, was really having as much trouble as Sophie said. Finally, Ann was skeptical that the doctor had gathered enough information to make such a frightening diagnosis. The doctor herself had said that all the blood tests and brain scans had come back normal. So what if Mike had become a little nervous during his interview and forgotten a few things? That could happen to anyone. He seemed fine today and Ann believed there were other reasonable explanations for the changes Sophie was so concerned about. Ann thought it was terrible that the doctor and Sophie would tell Mike something that would certainly only get him upset and make the situation worse.

The diagnostic feedback session is the first step toward accepting a dementia diagnosis. As Mike's story illustrates, however, it is not always an easy experience for any of the parties involved. No single test by itself reliably distinguishes early dementia from the nonprogressive memory problems that are common in old age. It is not unusual for family members to have different perspectives on how the person is functioning in his or her daily life, nor is it unusual for the affected individual to seem to do "better" in some situations or around some people. Memory problems and changes in comprehension that occur in the early stages of dementia may make the person with dementia unaware or even highly resistant to the diagnosis. Other medical conditions or essential medications being taken can further muddy the diagnostic picture. When there are alternative explanations for changes in thinking and behavior (such as Mike's bereavement) or inconsistencies in the history presented, a physician may treat for possible depression or some other coexisting medical problem, and then take a "wait and see" attitude that prolongs the family's uncertainty about what is really going on.

It is often prudent to delay giving a dementia diagnosis until some time goes by and clinical symptoms worsen. Occasionally, however, as in the case below, even the primary physician may be reluctant to discuss a suspected dementia diagnosis with patients and/or their families.[3]

Mr. and Mrs. Jones went to the doctor for an evaluation of Mr. Jones's memory. Several times over the past few months, he had gone to the grocery store and come home with nothing on Mrs. Jones's list. He had gotten lost during one of his morning walks and wound up asking for directions at a neighbor's apartment. He was uncharacteristically irritable and withdrawn at family events. The activities director at their retirement community took Mrs. Jones aside and expressed concern that perhaps her husband was showing the early signs of Alzheimer's disease. The doctor dismissed these concerns saying, "There's nothing wrong with him except the fact that he's had too many birthdays!" and sent Mr. and Mrs. Jones home with reassurances not to worry.

Why does something like this happen? Communicating a dementia diagnosis is difficult for some physicians because there are no definitive diagnostic tests, and medical treatment options are limited. These providers feel that there is no point in giving a diagnosis that you cannot do anything about. More common is the situation where very good doctors withhold a possible dementia diagnosis because they are simply not yet sure what is going on. Rather than revealing their suspicions, which may frighten or alarm the affected person or family, these doctors hold off until they have a chance to explore other possibilities such as treatment for depression, or until the person's decline is more evident. I have also seen primary physicians miss a dementia syndrome in someone they have known for years, even though it was obvious to me, a relative stranger. In these cases, familiarity and friendship collude against recognition of the problem: when the two meet, the physician overlooks subtle symptoms, and the person with dementia downplays his or her difficulties. Together, they wind up agreeing—"Nothing is wrong with you (or me) except too many birthdays!"

No one wants to hear that they, or a loved one, may have a chronic, progressive illness like Alzheimer's disease. Nevertheless, getting a diagnosis is an important step in the process for everyone involved. The manner in which you and your loved one are told about a suspected, or definitive, dementia diagnosis sets the stage for how you understand what to expect now and in the future. I feel that it is best for persons with dementia to be present when a dementia diagnosis is given. Meeting with the physician as a family gives you an opportunity to show your support for your loved one, and to make sure everyone's questions are answered. Although some family members fear their loved one will be very disturbed by it, most people accept the news calmly if it is delivered in a clear and compassionate manner. Having the diagnosis "on the table" makes it possible to begin the dialogue with your loved one about what he or she would want in the future when they need more help. It also allows the person with dementia and his or her family and friends to talk about priorities *now*; maybe it is time to take that trip to Hawaii or move into a smaller house, rather than putting things off to the uncertain future. Not telling persons with dementia about their diagnosis can lead to many problems. They become afraid that something, terrible but unknown, is wrong with them; they become paranoid that people are talking about them behind their back (often, this *is* the case); or they are cruelly shocked when some subsequent medical provider, who has not been let in on the secret, lets the diagnosis "slip" in an inopportune, careless fashion. You do not want that to happen to someone you care about.

If you are not satisfied either with the diagnostic evaluation your loved one received, or with the feedback you have had about the test results, I strongly urge you to contact your provider for more information or seek a second opinion elsewhere. Increasing numbers of health-care professionals are very knowledgeable and skilled in dementia diagnosis and treatment issues.[4] Do not hesitate to insist that your questions are answered to your full satisfaction. Medical providers are busy people, but in the long run, it is to their advantage to have a positive working alliance with you so that both of you can provide the best care possible to your loved one, both now, and in the future, when alternative long-term-care residential arrangements may be needed. If you live in an area with limited access to quality dementia assessment and referral centers, or where primary providers are not well informed about dementia care, you will need to take personal initiative to find the help and information you need. Much of that is available these days online; a number of excellent Internet resources for caregivers are listed in the Appendix at the back of this book, along with toll-free numbers for support services available through the Alzheimer's Association, national foundations, and state Division on Aging agencies.

ACCEPTING LIMITATIONS CAUSED BY DEMENTIA

Even caregivers who have fully accepted the fact that their loved ones have dementia sometimes have a difficult time accepting the ways in which the disease has changed him or her.[5] When people develop dementia, their cognitive and emotional changes usually occur gradually. Individuals with dementia also often insist that they are just fine. In fact, they have good days when their behavior is so normal that it seems to the observer that surely nothing is seriously wrong with their thinking. It is difficult to know what persons with dementia are still capable of doing on their own and when they need extra help. Think about your own situation. What changes have you seen in your family member with dementia? What changes do you think he or she would say have occurred? What kind of help do you both think is needed?

> Mrs. Yee was in our clinic with her two adult sons. The boys felt that their mother was "slipping a little." A professional businesswoman in the past, she still had many friends and activities, and was the primary caregiver for her husband who was disabled from emphysema and heart disease. Her sons were worried about Mrs. Yee's driving, and were concerned that she might be making mistakes with their dad's complex medication regimen. They wanted to hire a home health aide to come weekday mornings to help out, but both Mr. and Mrs. Yee were adamant that this was an unnecessary expense as well as an intrusion on their privacy. In their family, it was unthinkable that the sons would not respect their parents' wishes, no matter what fears they had for their safety.

As in the Yee household, you often find that every person living with dementia, whether patient or caregiver, has a different perspective on what has changed and what is needed to improve the situation. The person with dementia says, "I'm a little more forgetful than before but that doesn't interfere with my life at all"—even though you do see many examples of how it interferes! Children voice their concerns, but the demented person's spouse is highly protective and insists that the problems are not as bad as the children make them out to be. Sometimes, a distant relative, who has not seen your loved one in a long time, comes to visit and either sees many areas of decline that you have not noticed in your continual, daily interactions, or sees the person at his or her "best," and returns home to tell everyone in the family that you have been exaggerating Cousin Joe's decline. Who is correct? Who is seeing most accurately?

The answer is that all of these observations are correct, at least in part. We observed in earlier chapters that although dementia is progressive, its day-to-day effects can be very inconsistent. A person with dementia may have trouble performing an activity today that yesterday he did with ease. She may remember one appointment and forget the next. As caregivers, we may come to believe that these inconsistent gaps in ability occur because the person "just isn't trying" or "isn't motivated" or "is just doing things to annoy me." This is particularly true if, in the past, the person sometimes behaved in a similar way when he was not paying attention, or when the two of you were quarreling. Caregivers also, sometimes, have a "use it or lose it" mentality. They are afraid that accepting a loved one's limitations will lead to the caregiver doing things unnecessarily for the patient, and insulting the person with dementia while also causing extra work for themselves. Finally, especially in the earlier stages of dementia, caregivers are often shocked at the types of problems persons with dementia have. They simply cannot believe that mom really thinks her elderly husband is having an affair, or that dad does not understand that he should not be mailing out dozens of sweepstakes entries every week.

If you find yourself reacting in shock or disbelief like this, it is important to remember that no matter how similar the actions of persons with dementia are to how they acted in the past, their behaviors now do not have the same meanings or causes. Individuals with dementia are less and less capable of fully understanding the consequences of their deeds. Their disease may make them unable to remember decisions they have made, or unable to see how much they need help now from other people. They have difficulty finishing what they start, or starting things without guidance and support from people around them. They may say or do one thing when their intention was to do something totally different. Illogical, even crazy, ideas make perfect sense to them at times. Rapid changes in mood may occur. Although the person looks the same as always, and uses some of the same words and actions to express his or her feelings and desires, changes in the brain caused by dementia interfere with the ability to fully understand what he or she are doing. If you find yourself disbelieving that your family member's difficult or disturbing behaviors are dementia-related, you are not alone. This reaction is normal. Nevertheless, it will help you care for yourself and your family member more effectively if you can remember that he or she has decreasing control over his or her actions. Although remembering this will not stop you from getting angry sometimes or having feelings of resentment, embarrassment, or disappointment, you will get through these feelings more quickly.

Failure to recognize these brain changes in a person with dementia not only leads to increased stress in your relationship, but also potentially places the person with dementia or those around him or her in danger, as was the case with Chuck.

> Chuck respected his dad. As a kid, he had never liked him very much, though. "Pops" had been financially successful but overbearing and abrasive. It was no better now. His dad complained constantly. He was loud and rude to everyone he met. He was convinced he had cancer, although the doctors could not find anything wrong with him except that his memory was very bad. Although there was plenty of money to hire in-home help or even to put his dad in a home somewhere, Chuck felt he was the only one who could take care of his dad. Who else would take such a cantankerous old man? Chuck quit a job he loved so that he could be a full-time caregiver for his dad, but they fought constantly. Chuck hated how his dad was always ordering him around rather than taking care of things himself.

Chuck meant well in taking on solo care for his difficult father, but their situation was a catastrophe waiting to happen. Chuck was at risk of becoming a caregiver who mistreated his dad; he was isolated, depressed, and living with someone he had always considered obstinate and controlling. Chuck recognized that his dad could no longer live alone, but did not really appreciate the extent to which his father's cognitive impairment was affecting his behavior. In Chuck's mind, "Pops" was just being himself (only more so), and Chuck was still trying to get him to change. In the worst possible scenario, if this situation continued unchanged, Chuck might wind up abusing or neglecting his demented father.[6]

Not recognizing a demented person's impairments can have safety implications for other people as well. Is the grandmother with early Alzheimer's disease still able to care for an infant, while her daughter, a single mom, works during the day? Is the retired professor who continues to drive to the university across town still able to pay attention to the traffic signals and one-way street signs despite increasingly congested road conditions? Will someone like Mrs. Yee be able to deal appropriately with a medical emergency if her husband unexpectedly goes into respiratory arrest?[7] Every case is different and there are no simple answers to such questions. It is important, however, to regularly ask yourself whether it is realistic to expect your loved one to keep doing the things he wants, or you want him to do, and whether your expectations for yourself as caregiver are realistic as well.

ACCEPTING YOURSELF: IT IS NEVER TOO LATE TO GET BACK ON TRACK

As you learned in Chapter 1, resilient caregivers are able to reflect on past experiences in a way that leads to new understanding and new responses to the current situation. Madge is a good example.

Madge was a recovering alcoholic. With the help of Alcoholics Anonymous, she had quit drinking twenty years ago. Madge had many AA friends and felt that the organization had given her not only sobriety but also a way of approaching life that had made her a happier person and a better human being. I met Madge at a clinic where her husband was being treated for depression and agitation related to his Alzheimer's disease. In our first interview, Madge radiated peace despite her worry about her husband's situation. She attributed her ability to keep things in perspective to her years of following the AA philosophy: "living one day at a time, taking things as they are—not as I want them to be, balancing care of myself with care of others, and accepting the things I cannot change." Madge knew that as long as she was doing the best she could in caring for her husband, it was not necessary for her to handle every situation perfectly. In the grand scheme, things would turn out all right.

Over the years, I periodically saw Madge and her husband at the clinic. Even as her husband's symptoms progressed, leading to his institutionalization and eventual death, Madge continued to lean on her AA experiences and philosophy to help her negotiate the many difficult decisions she had to make. Each time Madge left my office, I felt like I should be paying her rather than the other way around. This is not to say that Madge had an easy time of it. She was frequently perplexed about what to do in a given situation, worried about how she would manage her husband's latest functional loss, and saddened and exhausted by it all. Yet, somehow, at her core was an abiding sense that in the end, "everything would turn out all right."[8]

Acceptance of what she could not change—her husband's diagnosis, his progressive clinical symptoms, and her own reactions and even caregiving mistakes—combined with a commitment to do the things she could to improve his care was at the core of what made Madge a resilient caregiver. The path to acceptance and commitment had, for her, come through embracing the AA philosophy. You do not need to be a member of AA, however, to be enthusiastic about the value of acceptance as a tool for improving psychological health. Acceptance-based therapeutic approaches have, in recent years, had a surge in popularity, and scientific conferences have been devoted to the topic.[9]

Although none of these treatment approaches have been systematically tested with caregivers, they have much relevance to the emotional challenges caregivers face. Unlike many modern-day cognitive therapies, acceptance-based approaches take the position that feelings do not have to change before you can do things differently.[10] For example, the caregiver with depression does not have to feel happy before she can go to an enjoyable family event. Rather, getting up and going out to do something fun will increase the likelihood that her feelings of depression will be lessened. Madge was a case in point. She had many feelings of worry, fatigue, uncertainty, and critical self-evaluations. Nevertheless, she did not let her inner reactions stop her from giving her husband the best care that she could at any point in time, even when that best care involved doing something she was very sad about, like moving him into a nursing home. It was not that Madge denied or minimized her negative thoughts and feelings. Rather, she accepted them—much as she accepted the aches and pains that came when she got out of bed in the morning—and kept going. As a result, Madge never got "stuck."

In contrast, Carol's inner experiences had become a real stumbling block to caring for her mother as she wished.

> Carol said she was so exhausted, she could barely move. She had promised her mom that she would not desert her when mom moved to a nursing home three months ago. Carol went to the nursing home every morning and usually spent the entire day there, helping her mother with all her meals, and seeing that her mother got the services she needed. She was continually having conflicts with the staff, who, she complained, were untrained, uncaring, and "not even Americans." At night, she would drag herself into bed, only to lie awake worrying about whether she should move her mother to a different facility. She knew she had been a terrible caregiver when her mother was at home. She wanted to make up for it now, but it was so hard since the nursing homes were all no good. What could she possibly do?

Carol had a lot of very strong opinions about herself, about what her mother needed and deserved, and about the facility where her mother was living. She was convinced that all of her opinions and reactions were literally true, and her attempts to fight against the incompetent staff and to make up for her own inadequate care when her mother was still at home had a desperate quality to them. No wonder. If Carol and all the facility staff were as bad as she said they were, it would be intolerable. However, Carol was so focused on her opinions that she was no longer fully experiencing the real world. She did not see the beautiful facility grounds, the gentle way the nurses' aides helped her mom to the shower, or how her mother laughed out loud when a custodian brought in her two Labrador puppies to visit. Carol had moved beyond pain; she was traumatized by her situation. What Carol needed was not to get rid of her negative opinions, but to give them a little less attention and credence so she could notice other feelings and observations as well. She needed to make contact with the bigger reality of her mother's care.

Madge had learned this skill and it was very empowering. It allowed her to be fully alive and present as she cared for her husband. Fully alive and present, of course, did not mean always peaceful or happy. Madge was a strong advocate for her husband, and not afraid to fight when it was needed to get her husband good care. However, Madge understood that although grief and suffering are part of caregiving, they are not the whole story. Her openness to both the good and the bad of her situation kept her from getting stuck. It helped Madge forgive herself when she was tired and snippy with her husband, allowed her to know when she had done all she could, and enabled her to see when it was time to move him into a nursing home. Madge's openness, her resilience, made it possible for her to grieve when he died, without giving up on her own remaining life.

The difference between Madge and Carol was not the severity of their caregiving situation or the intensity and frequency of their painful emotions. The difference was in Madge's perspective, which was less fixed and more fluid than Carol's. Have you ever seen the picture that is really two pictures in one? When you look at it one way, you see the outline of a vase, and when you look at it from a different perspective, you see two women's faces in profile, facing each other. The elements of the picture are always the same, but you can shift back and forth, sometimes focusing on the vase, and sometimes focusing on the faces. Carol and Madge could each focus on their feelings, reactions, memories, and opinions. However, Madge was also able to shift her focus to the values and guiding principles she had embraced in AA, which helped her to find purpose in what she was doing and experiencing. Life values are the "compass" that tell us which way to go, regardless of what we are thinking and feeling at the time. They are what make commitment possible. For Madge, her AA values were a touchstone she could always make contact with, regardless of what else was going on. Madge understood that it did not matter that she did not always live up perfectly to these values; all of us occasionally get caught up in the moment and lose sight of what gives our life meaning and joy. When you notice that happening, like Madge, shift your perspective back to your core values, to what really matters, what you want your life as a caregiver to be about. It is never too late for a resilient caregiver to get back on track.

SUMMARY

Acceptance of dementia is an important, even critical, aspect of becoming a resilient caregiver. We have identified three aspects of acceptance: accepting the reality of the dementia diagnosis, accepting the realistic limitations that dementia places on your loved one and on yourself, and lastly, accepting the complex cognitive and emotional responses that arise in caregivers as they carry out their role. Accepting the diagnosis is the simplest of the three. Although this can be challenging for caregivers, especially in the early stages of the disease, most caregivers will eventually get there. Once caregivers have accepted the fact that their loved ones have dementia, it is easier to have more realistic expectations for their behavior, as well as to be more realistic in the demands that they place upon themselves. Becoming realistic in your expectations, however, can take time, and usually has many ups and downs. This is because of the progressive nature of dementia. You become accustomed to the fact that your loved one cannot remember what day it is, but you are caught off-guard the first time he cannot remember who *you* are. You may have difficulty accepting the situation when your loved one resists your help in getting dressed but not the help of a paid home-health worker. Accepting limitations is a process of slowly letting go.

Accepting your own inner reactions to being a dementia caregiver is the most complex and difficult of all. It is different for everyone, but most people have times of irritation, resentment, impatience, and a whole myriad of reactions that they consider unacceptable to admit to others, or even to themselves. The problem is not that those reactions show up, but what you do with them. Caregivers who approach their role with a grim determination to handle it perfectly can become demoralized each time they fail to live up to their self-expectations. Their unwillingness to accept the difficulty they are having can lead them to unnecessarily delay asking for the help they need in providing care. Psychological acceptance—accepting the ups and downs of life as a caregiver—is also difficult because it is never-ending. No matter how practiced you become, as long as you live, there will always be something more to learn. Resilient caregivers learn to keep a loose rein on their inner selves, trusting that their core values and principles will guide them through in the end, no matter what challenges they face day-to-day.

◆ EXERCISE

Think of the problems that you are having with your loved one. How might things change if you accept the reality that he or she has a brain disease? Look at the example below.

Difficult behavior: My husband still wants to use the credit cards in his wallet but should not, because he has been running up huge charges that we cannot afford and buying things we do not even need. He has to stop spending so much money but I do not want to take away his cards because he will be angry and humiliated.

Acceptance: My husband thinks his judgment is still good, but his dementia has affected parts of the brain that help people think about future consequences of their actions, keeps them from acting impulsively.

We have talked about his credit-card bills many times, but because of his dementia, he does not always remember our conversations.

When we do talk about it, my husband agrees that there is a problem and says he will spend less. However, it is possible that even though he says the right things, because of his dementia he does not really understand as much as it seems. He can no longer agree to do something and then follow through.

The doctors say his dementia is progressive, so these changes are never going to get better, only worse.

Response: I can no longer expect my husband to be able to control his spending. Talking about it is not helpful. Even though I feel badly and I know it is going to make him upset, I need to stop his use of credit cards.

Your response is the hardest part! Once you accept that your loved one is not able to change a behavior because of his or her dementia, and once you accept that helping to solve the problem may be emotionally painful for you, then it will be easier to see the bottom line of what needs to be done. The challenge, of course, is to find a way to take action that is as respectful of your loved one as possible, and that helps him or her maintain dignity and self-esteem. In Chapter 5, we will talk more about creative problem solving. For now, pick a problem that you are having with your loved one, and go through the same process we did in the example.

My (loved one) is doing (describe difficult behavior).

_____

_____

I recognize that because of his or her dementia (describe how having a brain disease may be impacting your loved one's actions, in as many ways as you can think of. You may also ask your family or friends to help you think of some.).

_____

_____

I need to (given this perspective, how can *you* change to make the situation better?).

_____

_____

Chapter 4

N: NURTURE YOURSELF ◆

At this point in the book, you have learned how to take two important steps toward becoming a resilient caregiver. Instead of arguing with your loved one, you are trying to use other, more P.O.L.I.T.E., communication strategies. You have also taken steps toward a fuller acceptance of your loved one's dementia, which leads to more realistic expectations for both of you. Whew! Now it is time to take a break and spend some time focusing on *you*—what you need to do to nurture yourself. Taking care of oneself physically and emotionally does not always come easy for caregivers, as we see in the case with Joanne below.

Joanne was reluctant to take her husband Dick to visit a senior adult day program nearby. She did not think he would like it. She had visited the center on her own one day, and the participants seemed so much more demented than Dick. She watched the staff engaging them in activities Dick had never enjoyed, like singing old songs and doing craft projects. Everyone looked so old! Finally, their son convinced Joanne to just give it a try for one month. The first morning Joanne dropped Dick off, he begged her not to go, and a few blocks away she pulled the car over and cried. When she asked Dick later that day how he liked it, he said, "Not much. I don't want to go there." But after a couple of weeks of attending, Joanne noticed that on the mornings Dick went to the center, he was dressed and ready before the transport bus came, even though he usually had trouble keeping track of the days. The program staff reported that "Everyone loves Dick," and they had given him a special job helping water the potted plants throughout the building. Joanne, too, was noticing some changes. She felt less rushed because she knew she had a couple of days each week to run errands, go to her own medical appointments, or even just visit with girlfriends over coffee or on a walk around the neighborhood. At the end of the month, Joanne enrolled Dick for an extra day a week. She told her son, "I wish I had done this a year ago."

If you ask dementia caregivers what they regularly do "just to take care of yourself," many will find the question to be hilarious. Caregivers sacrifice a tremendous amount to provide quality care for their loved ones, and they often bear their responsibilities without help until their loved ones' dementia is very advanced. Over the years of doing clinical work, I have noticed there are many reasons why caregivers are sometimes slow to ask for assistance and are prone to neglect their own personal needs. In some cases, it is a desire to protect the feelings and dignity of the afflicted individual. Caregivers do not want to ask family and friends for help because they do not want their loved ones to be seen in such a state. Caregivers do not want pity, and they do not want to feel the discomfort or embarrassment of outsiders who do not really understand their situation. Better that the loved one be remembered in his or her prime.

Caregivers also want to protect other people. Children and friends of persons with dementia have their own jobs, marriages, children, taxes, yard work, and vacation plans. Caregivers are often reluctant to ask for help because they do not want to add to these individuals' burden. Caregivers want to be strong. They think they should be able to handle the situation themselves. Asking for help is reserved for only the most desperate circumstances. Some caregivers anticipate that if they ask for help, it will be denied or only reluctantly given, which somehow seems worse than never asking for help at all. Others decide that arranging for help is more work than doing without. When you rely solely on the kindness of others, and have to ask every week for a ride to church, or for someone to watch your loved one while you go to the dentist or take a walk, it is easy to decide that doing these things is not really that important.

Nevertheless, in order to stay resilient and maintain your quality of life in a "36-hour day," it is important to find ways to nurture yourself and get the help you need.[1] Have you ever flown on an airplane? When you are taking off, the flight attendants tell you that in the event of an emergency, you should put on your own oxygen mask before you try to assist the person next to you with theirs. If you're not thinking and functioning clearly, you're not going to be able to help anyone else. Caregiving is the same. What you specifically need to do to keep yourself thinking and functioning at your caregiving best will depend upon your unique situation. However, I can identify three general categories that cover most of the self-nurturing activities I have heard caregivers say they found helpful.

The first category has to do with nurturing your health. Doctors have a saying in medicine: "Check your own pulse first." If you are not taking care of yourself physically, emotionally, and spiritually, eventually you will not be able to sustain a resilient approach to caring for your loved one. The second way of nurturing yourself involves building regular respite breaks into your caregiving routines. It may seem paradoxical, but spending time apart is important for good relationships, not only for you but also for your loved one. The secret is in finding the right time, place, and person(s) for both of you to be with when you are apart, and we will talk about how to decide that. The third, and vitally important, way to nurture yourself requires learning to ask for the help you need. Most caregivers have people in their life who love them and want to help, but who just do not know what to do. For many of us, it is easier to give than to receive, and accepting help from others can be humbling. Asking for help, however, will help you stay connected to the world outside of dementia care, and it will also allow you to get those respite breaks and to nurture your health so you can continue to be the resilient caregiver you want to be.

NURTURING YOUR HEALTH

It seems wherever we turn these days, we are bombarded with admonitions to take care of our health. There are so many magazine and newspaper articles, television programs, and billboards reminding us to exercise, eat a careful diet, floss daily, and learn to relax that a person can become sick of hearing it. Caregivers say to me, "I know I'm supposed to do all these things but I don't have the time, energy, money, or inclination! Don't I have enough to worry about?!"

The problem with this common reaction is that neglect of your physical, emotional, or spiritual health is a slippery slope that, over time, can collapse into a deadly avalanche. In the beginning, neglecting your health does not seem to make that much of a difference. You may feel a little more tired than usual but it is easy to ignore. You may miss your weekly swim or the monthly book club, but you are nervous about leaving your loved one home alone. You may notice that you are putting on a few pounds or that your blood pressure has been creeping up, but you do not really feel sick enough to go to the doctor, and besides, what would he or she tell you that you do not already know? This pattern of thinking is completely understandable. Unfortunately, it is easy to overlook the fact that you are, little by little, wearing yourself out. A therapist friend uses this allegory to make the point:

A man was walking in the woods and came across an acquaintance trying to cut down a large tree with a saw. The first man said, "Hey, you look really tired! How long have you been at that?" His friend replied, "I am tired! I've been working on this tree for hours and it's not half done." The first man said, "Your saw is probably really dull by now. Why don't you take a rest, have something to eat and drink, and sharpen your saw?" But the man with the saw refused, saying, "I can't stop now, I have to get the tree cut down." So he just kept working away, trying to cut down the tree with a tool that no longer could do the job.

If you are a caregiver who has been neglecting your diet, exercise, health care, and social life, you are heading for exhaustion and probably not accomplishing all you want. It is like trying to cut down a tree with a dull saw. Caregiving is serious business. It is not unusual to meet someone who has been caring for a loved one for years, even decades. With children and other extended family members often living far away, there is not always someone readily available to lend a hand. Adding to the burden is the fact that many caregivers also have to work outside of the home just to make ends meet. Over time, the prolonged stress of caring for someone with dementia can take a serious toll on your physical and emotional health if you are not paying attention. Many studies have shown that prolonged caregiving increases one's risk for cardiovascular disease, weight gain, insomnia, vulnerability to infectious diseases, depression and anxiety, and even death.[2] Because of their increased risk for so many health-related problems, caregivers are sometimes called "the hidden patient" in dementia care.[3] One caregiver friend recently compared caregiving to running a marathon: "If you use up all your energy in the first few blocks of the race, you will never make it to the end. You need to pace yourself for the long haul." You have to *be* at your best if you want to *do* your best for your loved one, as we see in the story of Margaret.

Margaret was taking care of her mother who had Alzheimer's disease. Margaret herself had periodic episodes of rapid heart rate, dizziness, and an untreated ulcer. Her blood sugars and hypertension were skyrocketing. Although her mother's dementia was quite advanced, Margaret attributed the older woman's messy eating and difficulties with toileting to her mom being "stubborn." When the doctor told Margaret that she was in danger of losing her eyesight if she did not lose some weight and get her diabetes under control, it was a wake-up call. She applied for state assistance and was found to be eligible for eight hours/week of respite care for her mother. With the help of her physician and a nutritional consultant, Margaret started a sensible diet and an in-home exercise routine, and got appropriate treatment for her ulcer and elevated blood pressure. She went to a couple of Alzheimer's support-group meetings that had respite care, and met another woman caregiver who lived close by. The two of them became friends and started chatting on the phone for a few minutes each day. As Margaret began to feel physically better, she was less likely to yell at her mother's mishaps, and consequently, she started to feel that she was becoming a better caregiver. Margaret said, "I hadn't realized how sick I'd become and how much that was affecting my moods and reactions. Thank goodness I got some help before things got any worse. What would mom have done if I'd wound up blind or hospitalized?"

Like Margaret, a number of caregivers have told me that what finally got them taking care of themselves was the realization that it was selfish *not* to. It takes a real shift in perspective to realize that sacrificing yourself to the point where you make yourself sick is not really a very caring thing to do. Margaret came to understand that not only was she endangering her own health, but she was also not treating her mother very well because she felt so bad. With a little twinkle of humor, Margaret told me, "If mom were younger and could see the way I've been neglecting myself, she would kill me!" What would your loved one say to you? Chances are that your loved one would say that it is essential for you to become very proactive and give yourself at least some of the same quality attention and care that you are giving him or her.

NURTURING THE SELF WITH RESPITE

Once you make a conscious decision to start taking care of yourself, the very first challenge that will show up is making the time to do it. You have to find time that is yours alone. It does not have to be a lot of time, but it does have to be frequent and regular. It also does not necessarily always mean that you have to be physically away from your loved one, but it does mean taking breaks away from the attention, demands, and responsibilities that being a caregiver places upon you. Time is a precious commodity

for all of us, and that is especially true for caregivers of persons with dementia. There is so much that has to be done every day; how can you possibly squeeze in one more thing?

A counselor I know tells her clients to "find ten minutes every day doing
something that you love." Everybody, even the most frazzled caregiver, has
ten minutes to spare somewhere in the day if they are determined to find it
and use it well. When I first made this suggestion to a caregiver, her response
was that whenever she has a few extra minutes, she uses the time to lie down
and nap. Was that not enough? Surprisingly, what I have discovered is that
the answer to that question is "no"; although a little extra rest is a very good
thing for caregivers, by itself, it is not enough. I want to emphasize I am not
saying that caregivers shouldn't find ways to relax! A variety of meditation
and systematic relaxation strategies have been shown in research studies to
reduce stress in dementia caregivers,[4] and these are skills that I recommend
every caregiver should take the time to learn and practice (see Tips for
Learning to Relax).[5]

TIPS FOR LEARNING TO RELAX

- There are many different ways to relax. Using an audiotape
  or CD with a guided relaxation exercise, until you can reach
  deep relaxation easily on your own, is helpful when you are
  just getting started.

- Practice without using an alarm or clock. Settle in a comfortable place with no distractions. Plan in advance how to avoid
  or handle interruptions such as phone calls.

- Wear comfortable clothes and make sure your feet are warm.

- While you are learning to relax, sit in a comfortable, supportive chair. You may fall asleep while relaxing. If you find it
  happening every time, you may need to change the time you
  practice or use a different chair.

- Relaxation is a skill that your body must learn. Practice every
  day, at a time and place that works for you.

- Wait a couple of hours after eating since active digestion can interfere with relaxation.
- You may find your mind wandering. When you notice you are distracted, simply turn your attention back to your relaxation practice.
- Once you feel you have begun to learn to relax, try using relaxation in advance of everyday situations that you antici- pate may be stressful (such as a doctor's visit with your loved one). It is easier to control tension before it becomes intense.

However, taking time to relax does not replace the need to regularly do something you love, something that inspires and energizes you. If you are to thrive, not just survive, as a resilient caregiver, you need to nurture your spirit as well as your body. Doing something you love every day will help you stay in touch with the part of you that is creative, curious, and alive with a sense of the meaning of your life. Perhaps you are wondering whether anything meaningful can get done in ten minutes a day. Marcella taught me that a lot can happen in a little space of time.

Marcella lived with her husband, Larry, who had dementia caused by multiple strokes. Larry required a lot of attention; in addition to being forgetful, he had difficulty walking and transferring because of weakness on his right side, and he could not talk very well anymore. That was one of the hardest things for Marcella. She was gregarious by nature, and she missed having someone to converse with. One day, Marcella got a call from the daughter of an old friend, saying that the friend had been moved to a nursing home out of town following a fall in which she broke a hip. Marcella could not very well go and visit her friend, so she sat down and wrote a letter, which she inserted in a get-well card. To her surprise, about a week later, her friend wrote back. Marcella was de- lighted to hear from the friend, so she wrote another letter, and soon the two had a lively correspondence going. One day

Marcela and letters.

in a return letter, her friend shared with Marcella that her roommate was really lonely. Could Marcella write a letter to her, too? Marcella did. One thing led to another, and soon Marcella was writing to half a dozen residents in the nursing home. She loved getting letters in the mail, she loved how much her letters were appreciated, and she loved making new friends. If she sat down to write a letter and Larry needed something, she would put the letter aside and come back to it later in the day. Marcella told me that writing and getting these letters had given her a whole new lease on life.

Marcella was fortunate in that she stumbled across something that could be done in short chunks of time, as her schedule permitted, and that brought her tremendous pleasure and satisfaction. Although there were some days that Marcella never got around to picking up a pen, there were other days when she was able to spend more than ten minutes working on her letters, either because she had a longer stretch of time available to her, or because after being interrupted she would go back to them later in the day. Marcella liked the fact that she had something to do when she took a break that was more meaningful than watching TV. She also liked feeling that she was helping some people who were less fortunate than herself; as hard as life was for Marcella and Larry, at least they still had each other and were still in their own home.

Marcella found a way to nurture herself that suited her personality and situation. Perhaps you are wondering how you could find something comparable, something that *you* love enough to find time every day to do. While writing this book, I asked a number of caregivers what they love doing that (at least in principle) could be done for short periods of time. They gave me answers that fell broadly into three categories: (1) creating something beautiful (including knitting, crochet, needlepoint, cross-stitch, latch hooking, drawing, painting, mosaic work, carpentry, sanding, polishing, gardening, and playing piano); (2) being with people I love (spending time in person or over the phone with out-of-town friends and family, sending e-mail or letters, talking on the porch or over the fence with neighbors, having Bible study, coffee hour, or AA meetings at my

house, chatting with fellow hobbyists, and playing with and holding babies or small children); and (3) learning something new or keeping my mind active (watching educational TV or videos, reading, attending lectures at the community center or library, working the *New York Times* crossword, searching the web for information about caregiving, and listening to classical music). This is obviously not an exhaustive list, but just a reminder of the many things that you might consider making time for in your life.

If you still feel stuck, however, another way to begin to think about it is to ask yourself what makes life worthwhile? What gives my life meaning and purpose? What do I value most? One of my colleagues at the University of Washington, Dr. Rebecca Logsdon, has devoted much of her professional career to asking persons with dementia and their caregivers to rate their quality of life. Based upon what she has learned, Dr. Logsdon has created the Quality of Life in Alzheimer's Disease (QOL-AD) scale, which is included at the end of this chapter.[6] The QOL-AD asks caregivers to rate their own (or their loved one's) life across thirteen different domains, such as physical health, family, or ability to do things for fun.

Dr. Logsdon's research has shown that when a person's situation changes for the better (such as when a caregiver gets help in dealing with a loved one's challenging behaviors) or for the worse (such as in a move to a more restrictive living situation), how they rate their quality of life also changes. Depression and lack of involvement in pleasant activities negatively affect the ratings.[7] Conversely, when caregivers start to feel like they have more of those things that really matter in their life, their perception of their quality of life improves. When I first met Marcella, she rated her mood, friends, and ability to do things for fun as being "poor." Six months later, after she had established her letter-writing routine, she rated her mood and friends as "good." Marcella had picked a daily activity for herself that involved social contact, which was very important to her quality of life, and which she felt had become severely neglected since her husband had suffered his strokes. It is no wonder that a few minutes of letter-writing each day led to such improvements.

Marcella was fortunate to be able to do something she loved without having to leave home. That is not always possible, however. Sometimes, being able to do things you value and that nurture your soul requires getting physically away from your loved one. Jeffrey discovered that getting away now and then actually made the time he did spend with his wife more pleasant for the both of them.

> When Jeffrey put his wife, Alice, in the nursing home, it was a big adjustment. For years, he had taken care of all her needs, and now he had the big empty house to himself, with nothing to do. He did not much like it, so he went every day to the nursing home to be with Alice. He had been going for a couple of months and it still had not gotten any easier. Alice did not always recognize him, but when he would leave, Alice would cry and beg him to take her with him. One day, Jeffrey's old colleagues invited him to take a trip to attend a professional meeting out of town. Jeffrey almost refused but his kids convinced him that he should go. He had a wonderful time seeing old friends; one fellow even invited him to start doing some consulting work in his free time. Jeffrey enjoyed the extra money and the stimulation. Before long, he was going to the nursing home a little less often, several days a week instead of every day, and staying a little less long. The nursing staff encouraged him to spend the mornings and lunches with Alice, since she was so much brighter early in the day, and more easily distracted with other activities when he left, than if he came at night. Jeffrey was pleased with his new schedule. He worked those days and evenings that he did not go to the nursing home, so when he was there he was more relaxed and was able to enjoy himself.

Like Jeffrey, caregivers are often reluctant to take time away from their loved ones. This is even more the case when the person with dementia is still living at home. Many factors make getting away difficult. Some persons with dementia are very fearful of being separated from the caregiver, and become upset if the caregiver even leaves the room to take some laundry downstairs or to use the bathroom. In other cases, persons with dementia are unaware of their need for supervision, and so they become very antagonistic to anyone who appears to be there in the role of a "babysitter." Still others become increasingly suspicious as their dementia progresses, and suspect their caregivers of being involved in an affair if they leave the house unaccompanied for an hour or a day. In all of these situations, caregivers can feel that taking time for themselves while their loved ones stays with someone else would provoke an intolerable crisis. In the end, the caregivers just give up trying to get away.

What is tragic about these scenarios is that most of the time, a solution can be worked out. It is impossible to be happy to see someone when you are with him or her every minute of every day.[8] Wendy Lustbader, a social worker and therapist who has written widely about aging and caregiving, tells a story about taking care of her seriously ill mother-in-law. Wendy and her husband had given up most of their outside activities since becoming caregivers, and one day Wendy decided it had to change. She said "Barry, we can't take away her loneliness, and if we don't live while we take care of her, then we're waiting for her to die so we can live our lives again."[9] I related this story to a caregiver friend, who later told me,

> I've been thinking a lot about what you said about taking vacations and not waiting for someone to die. I'm taking a week off this month. And I've also noticed that my father-in-law is happy when one or both of us go out, too. I guess he doesn't want to die to get rid of *us* for a few hours either!

As this caregiver came to realize, being around different people and away from one another can be good for both you *and* your loved one, even though he or she may initially resist the change. The secret is finding the right amount of time to be away, the right place for your loved one to be when you are apart, and the right person(s) for both of you to spend time with instead of each other. How do you go about doing that?

It can be somewhat overwhelming trying to figure out what kind of respite option would be best for you and your loved one. Many factors go into this decision, including the size of the community you live in, and the type of formal and informal services that you have access to and can afford.

Probably, the most widely used formal respite alternative these days are adult day-health programs. A decade ago, Dr. Burton Reifler, a psychiatrist who has written extensively about Alzheimer's disease, published a paper extolling the virtues of such programs for older adults with dementia.[10] At the time this paper was published, the concept of adult day-care programs for persons with Alzheimer's disease was fairly new, and relatively few such centers existed. Today, adult day-health centers, supported by both private and public dollars, are abundant. Adult day programs are more than just a place to take your loved one so you can have a break. Although sites vary with regard to what specific services they provide, adult day-health programs usually have some combination of social and recreational activities, midday meals and snacks, exercise or movement therapies, physical and occupational therapy, nursing care, podiatry, assistance with personal care, and case management. Transportation is often available, and, increasingly, programs tailored for persons from specific ethnic, religious, or cultural backgrounds can be found. Many sites offer their services on a sliding scale, based upon your ability to pay. If your loved one seems understimulated or withdrawn—if he is spending much of the day sleeping or watching TV, or seems lonely or disinterested in his surroundings—an adult day-health program may be an excellent alternative for you, as we see in Ken's story below.

Ken had begun to wander, and it was very frightening for his daughter, Marilyn. On several occasions, he had left the house when Marilyn's back was turned or when she went to answer the phone. The last time it happened, it took the police a couple of hours to find Ken. Marilyn came to our clinic to talk about possibly putting her dad in a nursing home. Marilyn had two teenage daughters, and between keeping up with their demands and running the household, she just could not watch Ken every minute. When she was with him, it was usually to take care of something, like getting his lunch or helping him dress; Marilyn never had the time to just sit down and *be* with her dad. The social worker in our clinic encouraged Marilyn to check out an adult day-health program nearby. The staff member who came to their home to interview Ken and Marilyn seemed so kind and understanding, and so knowledgeable about how to talk to someone with dementia. She explained that wandering, in some cases, was caused by boredom, and that it sounded as if Ken was spending a lot of time just sitting by himself in his bedroom. Marilyn decided to give it a try. On Ken's first day at the center, there was a sing-along in the morning, and Ken spent part of his afternoon outside, helping to plant pansies in big flowerpots on the patio. He seemed to like it so much that soon Marilyn had him attending five days a week. Ken's wandering faded away; Marilyn discovered that many activities Ken enjoyed at the center also helped keep him occupied when he was at home. Marilyn was very relieved that, at least for now, she did not have to think about moving her dad after all.

Adult day-care programs, however, are not your only option. In-home helpers allow the persons with dementia to remain in their own homes when their caregivers are away or busy with other things. There are many different kinds of in-home assistance. Volunteer assistance available through community, school, or church programs can be very helpful for persons with little income, although you generally have fewer options with regard to when the helper can come and what kind of service they will provide for you. Alternatively, you can hire home health aides, housekeepers, visiting companions, live-in assistants, or certified nurses' aides. If you hire such helpers through an agency, it can save you the time and paperwork involved in verifying references to make sure the person is trained and reliable. The agency is responsible for supervising the individual, and can provide backup help in the event that your helper is sick or unavailable for some reason when you need him or her. Agencies also pay Social Security taxes, worker's compensation, and insurance fees, so you do not have to do it. Hiring in-home helpers yourself can be less expensive and may allow you more scheduling flexibility, but it can be more risky. In this case, it is up to you to screen the applicant, check his or her references, and negotiate task responsibilities, benefits, and rate of pay. You may or may not feel comfortable or qualified to handle this level of decision-making and day-to-day business oversight.

Another alternative is an overnight respite break outside of your home. Many assisted-living centers, adult family homes, and nursing homes provide short-term respite if they have any open beds available. This can be a perfect option if you want to get out of town for a weekend trip or a family event that your loved one would not be able to enjoy. It can also help caregivers who need a few quiet days to recover from an illness, or a couple of weeks to heal following a surgical procedure or hospitalization. I have had caregivers tell me that the use of such temporary respite services provided a nice transition between a time when they were perfectly able to care for their loved ones at home, and the time when they finally had to move him or her into long-term nursing care. It allowed both the caregiver and the care-recipient to become familiar with the facilities' staff and routines, and also gave the facility a chance to get to know the potential future resident in a less stressful context. Sometimes, adult day-health programs are based in facilities that offer such temporary respite, and your loved one can continue his or her usual daytime routine even while sleeping away from home. This kind of advance relationship building can greatly reduce the trauma for both you and your loved one if and when the day comes that you can no longer keep him or her at home, and until then, makes it possible for you to get away now and then without worrying over how your loved one is doing.

Information about how to identify, evaluate, and arrange for various kinds of community support services can be found in the Appendix to this book. I would particularly recommend contacting your local Senior In-formation and Assistance Program, which can be found either in your phone book or on the Internet. Every state in the nation has offices that provide this program. For no cost, they will provide you with listings of nearby agencies that hire home-health workers, as well as information about adult day-care-program sites and residential facilities that offer temporary respite care if you need a weekend off or need to go out of town for a few days. Staff at the local Alzheimer's Association can also assist you in de-termining what kind of respite service will be most appropriate for you and your loved one, and in identifying such services in your immediate area.

You should be prepared for the possibility that the first adult day center you look into, or the first person that you hire, may not work out. I have seen numerous instances in which a person with dementia rejects one in-home helper, but accepts another. One adult day-health program may not be able to handle your loved one if he or she begins to wander or becomes incontinent, whereas another program can manage these difficulties just fine. It can also take a while to figure out whether a person or place that offers respite services is the right one for you and your loved one. Care-givers commonly tell me that their loved ones complain about going to the adult day-care center, but then, when the caregiver drops in unexpectedly or talks to the day-care center staff about how things are going, it seems that the loved one is having a wonderful time while they are actually there. Consistency is very important; persons with dementia have difficulty ad-justing to any change in routine, but if you give it a reasonable time (e.g., a one-month trial period), things may settle down. If one situation does not work out, do not give up! The next person or place you try may work beautifully.

NURTURING YOURSELF BY LETTING OTHERS HELP YOU

Formal respite services such as adult day-health programs and in-home care have helped millions of caregivers and their loved ones. However, not everyone wants, or is able, to use them. For these caregivers, respite may come from informal sources of help such as family and friends. In fact, even those caregivers who do use formal services almost always need more and different kinds of assistance than those provided by even the best agency or community program. So where is that assistance going to come from? In a sense, it is going to come from you! You are going to ask people in your life to help you.

As I said earlier, most persons with dementia, and their caregivers have people in their lives who love them and want to help, but who just do not know what to do. Yet, I see many caregivers who do not ask for the help that is waiting to be given. Why is that? In my clinical practice, I have seen two main reasons. First, caregivers do not want to ask for help; they want to be able to handle things themselves. Second, caregivers often do not know what to ask others to do for them. Have you ever felt either of these things? If you can find a way to get beyond your hesitation to ask for the help you need, you may be surprised at what a positive difference it makes.

Not Wanting to Ask for Help

Asking for help can be hard. When you ask someone to help you, you face the possibility that they may say "no." You may be afraid that they will be silently critical of you because you need help and cannot manage on your own. You may not know what to say, particularly to people with whom you do not have a long-standing, intimate relationship. In other cases, the people to whom we feel closest can be the hardest ones of all to ask for help. Let us see what Lucille had to say.

> Lucille and her husband Tom, who had Alzheimer's disease, had moved into a small basement apartment owned by their son, Dan. Dan would regularly ask, "Is there anything I can do to help you?" Lucille would always reply, "Nothing— unless you can get rid of your dad's memory problems. There is nothing else we need." No matter how often Dan asked, Lucille always gave the same answer, even as she grew more tired and depressed, helplessly watching Tom slip away.

When I met Lucille, she and Tom had been living with Dan for almost a year. Although Lucille was grateful to Dan, she also felt very overwhelmed. However, she was reluctant to admit this to her son. She did not want to burden him; Dan had already given up his privacy and extra space, and asking for more seemed ungracious. She did not want to leave Tom because she was afraid Dan might become impatient with his dad, or get distracted and not notice if his dad needed something. Lucille felt a little embarrassed that she was having trouble keeping their tiny apartment clean, but did not want to ask Dan to help her with something she should be able to do herself. And occasionally, although this was very hard to admit, Lucille wished that Dan would just see what needed to be done and do it, rather than putting her in the uncomfortable position of asking for help. "Dan sees me struggling to get his dad cleaned up after breakfast; if he really wants to help, why doesn't he stop reading the morning paper and just do it?"

The confusion and mixed feelings that Lucille expressed have been repeated over the years in conversations with many caregivers. Lucille needed help, but she did not want to bother her son; she believed she was the only one who could take good enough care of Tom; she did not want her son to know that she was having a hard time; and she resented the fact that her son did not take care of things without her having to ask. The truth was also that Lucille did not really want to acknowledge to herself how much she needed Dan's help. For some caregivers, accepting that they cannot do it alone means coming face to face with the reality that someone they love is declining and is not going to get better. Although it was misguided, Lucille's reluctance to let her son know what a hard time she was having was her way of trying to maintain some kind of normalcy in her life and her marriage.

For many of us, like Lucille, it is easier to give than to receive, and accepting help from others can be humbling. It may be easier to accept help if you can realize that accepting help is a gift to the giver as well as to you. It builds intimacy by giving the giver a deeper appreciation of what life is like for you and your loved one with dementia. It also gives them a chance to show the stuff that they are made of, the courage and compassion that others may not realize they have. Dakota and her husband were a case in point.

Dakota and her husband, Matthew, were not typical dementia caregivers. They were young, and a toddler was straddled over Dakota's hip. They were both covered with tattoos and had body piercings in many places. They had little money, and lived in a tiny house in a low-rent part of town. Their family objected when the couple decided to pull Dakota's grandma out of the nursing home and bring her home to live with them. Grandma had been at the nursing home for a year, and had stopped walking and talking and was losing weight. Dakota thought she and Matthew could do better by grandma, although everyone else thought they were too young and it would be too much work. Happily, when I met them, grandma *was* doing much better. She loved having her great-grandson crawl over to her and stand up on her chair. She liked petting the old white cat that would jump into her lap after dinner. Dakota had her grandma doing chair exercises with morning TV shows, and she seemed to be getting stronger. She certainly smiled a lot when I talked to her. Dakota cared for her grandma like an extra young one in the house, protective of her safety but putting her smack dab in the middle of everything that was going on. Dakota and Matthew wanted to know if they were doing everything they could. I assured them they were doing a great job.

At the beginning, no one imagined that this unusual young couple would be the best thing that could happen to Dakota's grandma. It is easy to underestimate the power of love. Dakota and Matthew were very proud of all they had accomplished. Being allowed to take care of grandma had given them a sense of competence and self-worth that no one would ever be able to take away. Is it possible that there is a friend or family member somewhere in *your* life who is waiting to help? If so, you should not be afraid to ask; your asking for help may, in reality, be giving someone a chance to rise up and be their best, as it did for Dakota and Matthew.

Not Knowing What to Ask For

The other big reason caregivers often do not ask for help is that they simply do not know what kind of help they really need or whom they should ask. The best way to figure out what kind of help you could use is to make a list of the many things you do for yourself and your loved one.

For example, what is a typical day like for you? Does your loved one need help with preparing meals or eating, dressing or showering, or personal hygiene such as shaving? Does he or she need some new socks or a pair of sweatpants that you have not had time to run to the mall and pick up? What kind of chores do you have around the house? How often do you vacuum the rugs, make the beds, wash the windows, do the laundry, sweep the sidewalk, clean the kitchen and bathrooms, or buy groceries? Are there any home repairs that you have been putting off until you find the time? Are there any dripping faucets, furnace filters that need replacing, or does the car need an oil change? Are there rooms that need painting, roof gutters that need the leaves cleaned out, or a lawn that needs mowing? Perhaps you need to make a doctor's appointment, or balance the checkbook, or buy a present for your nephew's birthday. Are there ever days that you wish you could leave your loved one at home while you meet friends for coffee or go to a caregiver's support group? Maybe you just wish there was someone other than you for your loved one to talk to or watch TV with while you fold the laundry in the next room. The list could go on and on. Almost everything you do could potentially be delegated to another person, at least now and then.

Some of what you could ask for is a one-time request, like painting the guest room of the house. Other requests are seasonal, like cleaning gutters or shoveling snow. Still others could be ongoing, like having a few hours of respite every Saturday morning, or having your garden weeded or lawn mowed every month. Remember, everything that you let someone do for you, you do not have to do yourself. You may have to give up a little control; when other people help us out, they often do things differently than we would. For example, your grandson may not be quite as neat as you are with the lawn trimmer, or you may not like the fact that your daughter does not polish the copper pans when she does the dishes. Over time, however, you may find that either these things do not really matter all that much, or the people who are helping you will do your chores the way you want them done if you just tell them. One adult daughter told me she was shocked to discover that her caregiver mother had always refused help with the laundry because she ironed her demented husband's boxer shorts and bed linens. The mother assumed that her daughter would think this was silly and would not do it properly, when in fact, her daughter was happy to do the extra ironing once she understood it was important to her mom. However, even if you discover that your helpers cannot be "trained" and some things you must do yourself, chances are that there are plenty of other areas where you could still use a hand.

Some caregivers have no trouble recognizing what they need done, but it is harder to know *whom* to ask for help. The best way to figure this out is to make a list of everyone in your life you have regular (say, at least monthly) contact with. A typical list would include adult children and other extended family, neighbors, friends, church acquaintances, coworkers, or fellow service organization members or school alumni. Now, take the list of possible activities you prepared earlier that could be delegated—things you do in the course of a day, home repairs, chores, yard maintenance, and so on. Compare this with the list you just made of people you know. Sometimes there is an obvious choice; the next-door neighbor who works with computers may be happy to help you figure out why your e-mail is not working. The nephew who is a builder could get up on the roof and check out your shingles before the winter rains come. Whom you ask will depend, in part, upon whether you have a one-time request like pruning the roses, or something ongoing like having your prescriptions picked up at the pharmacy. It will depend on whether the job is one that could only be done by someone you trust completely, like depositing your Social Security check at the bank. Just for fun, try to assign every person you have listed with at least one item on your list of needs. What did you come up with?

SUMMARY

Nurturing yourself is an essential aspect of being a resilient caregiver. You cannot take care of someone else when you are not taking care of yourself as well. There are many reasons why caregivers have a difficult time taking care of themselves. Caregivers do not want to be a burden to others. They may be concerned that friends and family will not understand what their loved ones are going through, and will not treat them with the dignity and respect they deserve. Sometimes, caregivers are embarrassed—either about the loved one's behavior or about the fact that they need help. They may be concerned that help will be given grudgingly, or with silent criticism. They may just be worn out and might not want to deal with the hassle of getting help.

Although all these concerns are reasonable, the fact remains that you need to take care of yourself if you are going to be resilient and want to maintain your quality of life. You need to take care of your physical, emotional, and spiritual health. This is not indulgence—it is essential if you are going to continue to provide the care that you want to give to your loved one. You need to build in regular times to be away from your caregiving responsibilities. To accomplish all this, you are going to need to learn to ask other people for help. Help can come from formal support services such as adult day-health programs, in-home services, or residential programs that offer respite care. You will also, almost certainly, need to learn to ask for help from the nonprofessionals in your life: your family, friends, neighbors, and community associates. Getting the help you need will keep you from becoming isolated and will make it possible for you to do the things you need to do to be resilient and healthy. Both you and your loved one deserve nothing less.

◆ **EXERCISE**

Complete the Quality of Life in Alzheimer's Disease scale below (Table 3), answering it for your loved one. How would you rate your loved one's physical health? His or her energy? Mood? After completing the scale for your loved one, answer it for yourself.

How many items have you rated "poor" or "fair" for your loved one and yourself, and how many have you rated "good" or "excellent"? What does this tell you? When they think about their lives this way, many caregivers discover that they and their loved ones have a good life, despite the limitations they experience from living with a dementing illness. If this is true for you, congratulations!

If it is not true—if you have mostly "poor" or "fair" ratings on these quality-of-life domains—is there anything you can think of that could change to improve the situation? Are there things that you could change for the better in your friendships, your family, your involvement with

TABLE 3. Quality of Life in Alzheimer's Disease (QOL-AD)

Please rate your loved one's situation, as you see it. Circle your responses. Now, rate your *own* situation, putting a check in each box beside the correct response.

1. Physical health	Poor	Fair	Good	Excellent
2. Energy	Poor	Fair	Good	Excellent
3. Mood	Poor	Fair	Good	Excellent
4. Living situation	Poor	Fair	Good	Excellent
5. Memory	Poor	Fair	Good	Excellent
6. Family	Poor	Fair	Good	Excellent
7. Marriage	Poor	Fair	Good	Excellent
8. Friends	Poor	Fair	Good	Excellent
9. Self as a whole	Poor	Fair	Good	Excellent
10. Ability to do chores around the house	Poor	Fair	Good	Excellent
11. Ability to do things for fun	Poor	Fair	Good	Excellent
12. Money	Poor	Fair	Good	Excellent
13. Life as a whole	Poor	Fair	Good	Excellent

© Modified from R. G. Logsdon, 1996; used with permission.

household activities or things you are doing to take care of your or your loved one's health? Are there activities that you love that you have been neglecting and could start doing "ten minutes a day?" Are there people you could be asking for help in the next month to improve your or your loved one's quality of life? Write down their names and make a commitment to call them in the next week to get the help you need.

Chapter 5

C: CREATE NOVEL SOLUTIONS

We have seen how resilient caregivers can learn to stop arguing and use more effective communication strategies with their loved ones, accept the real limitations a dementia diagnosis places on them, and nurture their own physical and psychological health. Even after you do all this, however, you will likely still be faced with unexpected and unusual situations that catch you by surprise and that need to be handled. With dementia, almost anything can happen! In this chapter, we will talk about the importance of creativity in reducing the frequency, severity, and duration of dementia-related behavior problems. In the story below, Mary gives us an example of the creative problem solving that characterizes resilient caregivers.

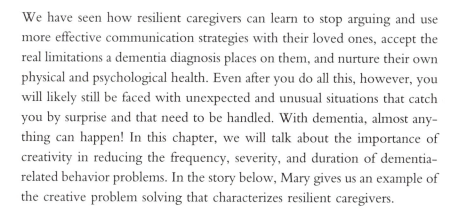

Lois still lived alone with a lot of help from her adult children in town. Her daughter, Mary, lived nearby and came by daily to take Lois to spend the afternoon and evening with Mary's family. The arrangement generally worked well, with one exception. Every morning after Lois got up, she would start calling Mary's house. By that time, Mary, her husband, and the kids were at work and school, so Lois would leave a message: "What time are you coming by? Should I bring anything? Can you take me to the bank? Will you take me to get groceries?" A short while later, Lois would forget that she had already called, and would dial Mary again, leaving the same message. This happened over and over each day, filling up Mary's home voice-mailbox and making it impossible for anyone else to leave messages for the family.

To solve the problem, Mary got a second phone line and gave the new number to all the other family and friends. She then changed the outgoing message on the old number to this one: "Hi, Mom! This is Mary. I'm coming to pick you up at two this afternoon. You don't need to bring anything. I'm going to take you to the bank on the way home. We can also stop by the grocery store and pick up anything you need. See you soon! I love you!" Each time Lois would call, she would listen to Mary's message and then hang up. This arrangement worked well for some months, although Lois did complain to Mary's sister, Sally, that "Whenever I call your sister, I can never get a word in edgewise!"

Human beings are largely creatures of habit and repetition. Our ability to recognize patterns, to find the most efficient way to do things, and then to keep doing them that way enhances productivity and frees up our minds to pursue other interests. This is also true in relationships. Over years of living together or knowing someone well, families develop ritual ways of doing things that are familiar and that serve to keep households running more or less smoothly.

Unfortunately, when dementia enters the picture, the rules begin to change. In the beginning, it is not difficult to compensate for dementia-related memory loss with new routines: written reminders, scheduled activities, and stable environments. Indeed, a consistent and predictable daily routine is a tremendous help to persons with dementia at almost every stage of the disease. As dementia progresses, however, problematic situations often arise that are unsafe, disruptive, or just plain annoying and not easily solved with simple routines. As in the example above with Mary and Lois, these problems are often unique to you and your loved one; there is not a book in the world that will tell you what to do in every situation. You have to put on your thinking cap and figure out a solution that is loving and respectful, and also works. Rationally pointing out to Lois that she has already called ten times that day, and that Mary comes every day to help her with her errands, probably would not have prevented Lois from calling again, although that might have worked perfectly in the past. In fact, trying to persuade Lois to alter her pattern of daily phoning might not only have been ineffective but also have caused her to become angry or to feel hurt because it might seem that Mary did not want to talk to her anymore. Like the dancer who must follow her partner's lead to get across the room, Mary needed to find another approach.

This chapter will discuss what creativity means in the context of solving dementia-related behavior problems. Several aspects of creativity will be described, and we will look at how these relate to a common situation that many caregivers face. I will then describe two approaches to problem solving that can be used to foster creativity as you deal with your loved one's more idiosyncratic behavioral challenges. The first invites you to build upon your loved one's past experiences and actions to figure out what may be contributing to problem behaviors and how they might be solved. In the opening pages of Section II, we saw how Bob got his wife Margie to shower by taking advantage of the fact that both of them had always loved ballroom dancing. Your loved one's previous likes and dis-likes, work and hobbies, personality traits, and successes and traumas all may provide clues as to what kind of creative intervention might be helpful in resolving your unique problem, and, conversely, what might not only be unlikely to work, but also actually make the situation worse.

The second strategy for enhancing creative problem solving focuses on learning to step back and take a look at the larger, immediate context in which difficult, dementia-related behaviors are occurring. It may seem as if your loved one's problem behaviors are occurring out of the blue, without any rhyme or reason to them. My experience, however, is that that is rarely the case. Human beings, even those with a brain disease like dementia, do not live in a vacuum. We are all impacted every moment by a web of influences that may be as mundane as the temperature of the room or as complex as the lifelong habit of avoiding other people when we are afraid or angry. In this chapter, we will learn a systematic way to try to identify persons, objects, or events in the immediate moment or environment that may be triggering your loved one's difficult behaviors. We will also look at things that you or other people do in such instances that may be making the situation better or worse. Experts in dementia care have developed an approach called the ABCs of behavior change, and there is a large body of research showing its effectiveness. Together, we will see how you can learn to use this approach—building upon lessons in communication, acceptance, and nurturance that we have already discussed—to come up with creative solutions for whatever situation arises in your daily life with your loved one.

WHAT IS CREATIVE PROBLEM SOLVING, ANYWAY?

Perhaps you are thinking to yourself, "I'm not a very creative or imaginative person. I don't think I can do this." Yes, you can! In this context, the term creativity—like resilience—describes a set of skills that can be increased over time with practice. As such, creative problem solving has several aspects worth considering. First, *Creativity arises out of need.*[1] In other words, human beings are most likely to be creative when there is a problem to be solved and the usual, obvious solutions are not working. Caregivers rarely call or come into my clinic when things are going fine. Instead, I am likely to see them when they need help thinking of something new to try. If you sometimes feel "stuck" dealing with your loved one, as in the example with Jose below, you have already taken the first step toward creativity by acknowledging that a new approach or solution is needed.

> Jose lived with his mom and dad, both of whom had Alzheimer's disease. He had to work his retail job during the day but there was no one else to stay with them. When I asked how he managed, he said, "Oh, I have a system! I turn off the gas and the electricity, and let them putter around the house all day until I get home. The neighbors keep an eye out and check in a couple times a day. I alarmed the front gate so if mom or dad try to leave, someone is likely to hear and come help get them back home."

Jose wanted his parents to be able to stay in their own home. He did not believe that outsiders should be involved in their daily care, and he was the only one in the family who had offered to help out. Jose was also concerned about money. Paid in-home help was too expensive, even if he had wanted to arrange it. Given what seemed to be the realities of the situation, Jose had shown considerable ingenuity coming up with a plan to help his parents. The plan raised some significant safety concerns, but he did not know what else to do. He needed some new ideas. This leads to the second aspect of creative problem solving, that is, *Creative thinking involves looking at your situation from different viewpoints.* Do you remember the old Hindu fable about the six blind men and the elephant?[2] Each blind man was touching a different part of the elephant—its tusk, tail, trunk, side, ear, or leg—and so each had a very different assessment of what an elephant was like. Like the blind men, all of us try to make sense out of our situations based on what we see or understand, but sometimes in the process, we make interpretations that are misguided or incorrect.[3] Concerns about money and family pride had, up to this point, kept Jose from seeking out community services for his parents, but now he was willing to consider some alternatives. He just needed some help getting started.

The Nobel Prize–winning chemist Linus Pauling has been quoted as saying, "The best way to get a good idea is to get lots of ideas." However, it can be difficult for us to look at things from different viewpoints and get lots of ideas by ourselves because, like Jose, the ideas we have are so familiar and often tied to strong, long-standing beliefs. This leads us to a third aspect of creative problem solving, which is, *Trust the group process,* or more familiarly, *Two heads are better than one.* By coming to talk to me, Jose was inviting my perspective on his situation. I knew of senior resources Jose had never heard of. He began to talk to coworkers and friends to get additional ideas besides mine. Eventually, Jose found a nearby program that provided supervised activities and a midday meal for persons with dementia. Fees were on a sliding scale that he could afford two days per week. Jose also enrolled his mom and dad in a Meals-on-Wheels program that brought hot lunches on days they were at home. Both of these activities supplemented the safety net of persons looking out for Jose's parents when he was at work, and also improved their psychosocial and nutritional well-being.

I had suggested that Jose involve his large extended family more in caring for his parents, but Jose was not interested in pursuing this. His rationale was that they were all busy with families of their own, and he did not want to burden them. Besides, it made Jose feel good that he was handling things his way. This illustrates another important aspect of creative problem solving, which is, *You want lots of ideas but you do not have to use them all.* A friend of mine describes this process as "sampling." Just as when you go to a dinner buffet and pick and choose what looks good to try and what to pass by, so too with brainstorming ideas. What is critical is generating as many ideas as possible, so you have multiple options to try. Which option(s) you actually select is less important. You can always try something else if what you pick does not work. And you never know what will work until it is tried! I have many times been surprised at the choices caregivers made from a brainstorming list, and sometimes an idea that I thought was the "worst" one worked perfectly well. You are the expert on taking care of your loved one. Once you have ideas and choices, you will be able to figure out how best to use them.

The final aspect of creative problem solving to remember is that *You are more likely to be creative in the future when it has been successful in the past.*[4] That means you have to give it a try! Everything is difficult before it becomes easy, and creative problem solving is no exception. The discomfort or skepticism you feel when you begin to experiment with behavioral problem solving is normal, but things do get easier over time. I realized this had happened to Jose when, a couple of months after visiting our clinic, he came home from work and found that his dad had fallen and no one had been around to help pick him up. Jose realized that if his parents were going to be able to stay in their own home, he was going to need some additional family support. Whereas before he had been reluctant to ask his siblings for help, he now talked to each of them individually, explained the situation, and asked what they could contribute to their parents' care. Together, the family was able to pull together the extra money to increase their parents' attendance at the adult day-care center to four days per week. Jose arranged to have the adult day-care van deliver his mom and dad to one of his several sisters' homes, who would watch them until Jose got off work and came to pick them up. His sisters also had their parents over on days that Jose worked and the parents did not attend adult day care. What had seemed impossible a few months earlier had all worked out. Jose was proud that together his family had accomplished so much, and felt confident that they would be able to handle future challenges as they came along.

APPLYING CREATIVE PROBLEM SOLVING: TWO BRAINSTORMING APPROACHES

In Jose's story, we saw that creative problem solving is really nothing more than coming up with new ways of doing things and seeing what happens next. As you begin to practice looking at problem situations from different perspectives, brainstorming novel solutions, and giving some of these solutions a try, you will be well on the way to becoming resilient in whatever dementia-related challenges you and your loved one face. As in the case of Jose, however, coming up with novel solutions is not always easy, even when you enlist the help of other people. Thinking about the following approaches to problem solving may help get you moving when you feel you have run out of new ideas to try.

Problem Solving: Learning from the Past

There is an old expression that says, "As people age, they become themselves, only more so." Over a lifetime of practice, our habits, idiosyncrasies, tendencies, reactions, and beliefs tend to become more consolidated and more deeply entrenched into patterns. Many of these patterns are delightful. How many older persons have you met whose deeply lined faces reflect a lifetime of easy laughter, or whose calm eyes reflect the serenity and wisdom of their age? Other patterns may not be so pleasant. In Charles Dickens's well-known story, *A Christmas Carol*, Mr. Scrooge becomes more and more miserly, opinionated, and cantankerous as the years go by, and acquisition of money comes to dominate his every waking hour. I have had caregivers tell me that they feel like they are living with Mr. Scrooge. Although it does sometimes happen that people with dementia have a personality change for the better, more often it is the undesirable traits of our loved ones' younger years—their anxieties, irritability, suspiciousness, or lifelong habits—that become exaggerated and underlie difficult dementia-related behaviors.

We have already discussed how acceptance on the part of the resilient caregiver plays a major role in coping with difficult behaviors that are exaggerations of lifelong personality characteristics or routines. However, reflecting on the historical experiences, habits, and interpersonal patterns of persons with dementia can also help caregivers understand what their loved ones must be experiencing. Imagine how painful it would be for a competent adult to discover one day that he can no longer remember how to knot his tie, or that she cannot figure out how to run the dishwasher. How frightening would it feel to begin to lose a sense of time and place, so that the past seems as real and alive, maybe more so, than the present? As we see in the case below, if you can put yourself in your loved one's shoes, you will likely find a deep compassion for what he or she is going through, and that may help you figure out how to help the patient.

> Mrs. Katz was a Holocaust survivor who lost her parents, siblings, and extended family in the war. After her husband died, Mrs. Katz moved in with her youngest daughter, Gertrude. Gertrude brought Mrs. Katz to the doctor because her mother was becoming increasingly difficult to manage. Several times, Gertrude had come home from work and found household furniture moved outside onto the front lawn, and her mother hiding inside the locked house. Once when the pizza man came to the door, Mrs. Katz started screaming and striking him with her fists. She refused to let her grandchildren open the living-room curtains or answer the telephone when it rang. She accused Gertrude and her son-in-law of trying to poison her, and refused to eat. The doctors tried several medications but none seemed to help. Mrs. Katz's increasing fearfulness, paranoia, and aggressive outbursts continued to worsen until her daughter moved her into a residential home that specialized in caring for aging Jewish

individuals who had survived the horrors of World War II. In that calm, quiet environment, surrounded by Judaic art, caring staff, and the quiet rhythms of weekly Shabbat rituals and subdued seasonal holidays, Mrs. Katz gradually stabilized, and was cared for until she died several years later.

Mrs. Katz, in her dementia, was reliving the terror of her past wartime experiences. Her children and health-care providers understood the source of her escalating behavior. Although they were not able to find a medication or behavioral solution that allowed her to remain at home, their insight did lead them to search for a residential alternative that was specifically set up to deal with and help persons like her.

In less extreme situations, the right background information can lead to both increased understanding on the part of the caregiver and practical ideas for solving the problem. For example, the owner/operator of a small board-and-care home told me this story:

Mr. T was a nighttime wanderer. He would get up a couple of times a night and try to exit the house. Fortunately, the doors were alarmed, so that when he opened one, the alarm would awaken the staff person sleeping there, and he or she would get up and stop Mr. T from leaving. Unfortunately, the alarms also woke up the other residents in the house, all of whom (including Mr. T) were upset about the noise and had to be calmed down to go back to bed. Nobody in the house was getting any sleep. The owner called Mr. T's family to tell them he would have to move. In the course of the conversation, it was discovered that Mr. T had a lifelong pattern of checking the doors in the house before he went to bed. If he got up during the night to use the bathroom, he would go through the house and again check the doors before returning to bed. The owner realized that Mr. T had not been trying to leave her home at night; he had simply been "checking" the doors as had been his routine, and in the process of doing so, was setting off the alarms. They worked out a plan where a monitor was placed in Mr. T's room that quietly alerted the staff when he got out of bed at night. The staff person would help Mr. T to the bathroom and turn off the house alarm. Together they would then go from door to door to check the locks, Mr. T would go back to bed, and the staff member would reset the alarm system. Although there were occasional accidents where Mr. T got up without the staff hearing him and set off the alarms, they were no longer worried that he was trying to wander away, and Mr. T was allowed to stay at the home.

Finally, knowledge about a person's past can sometimes offer clues about activities for your loved one that may distract or interfere with problematic behaviors. For example, one caregiver told me that his demented mother had the annoying habit of singing incessantly in the car when they were driving. He knew that, in the past, she had always had a sweet tooth. He found that offering his mother gum to chew when they rode together both satisfied her craving for sweets, and at the same time made it impossible for her to sing. In another example that follows, a patient's work history was the key to reducing her agitation.

Dr. Margaret Lyle was a retired family-medicine physician who had advanced Alzheimer's disease. While her husband was recovering from hip surgery, he placed Dr. Lyle in a medical rehabilitation unit that offered prolonged respite stays for persons with dementia. Dr. Lyle was very upset about being there and was highly disruptive on the ward. A couple of days after Dr. Lyle was admitted, the head nurse gave Dr. Lyle a clipboard and asked her if she would like to join the nurse on her morning rounds. Together, they went around to each resident's room, asked about how he or she was doing, and then went back to the nurse's station where the head nurse did her charting. The same process was repeated at the end of the day, and then twice everyday thereafter. Soon, Dr. Lyle was accompanying the nurse on her other activities around the unit as well. Dr. Lyle's disruptive agitation disappeared; she was content as long as she was "working." All the residents and staff became very fond of her.

In both the examples above, understanding a person's past experiences and habits provided a clue to how best to help them in the present. At other times, however, your loved one's behavioral changes may seem to be very inconsistent with the person they used to be, and you cannot figure out what to do. In such cases, it is often helpful to look at the immediate context in which the problems are occurring in order to discover a creative intervention to try.

Problem Solving: Learning the ABCs of Behavior Change

In my research work at the University of Washington, I have talked to many caregivers who complain that their loved ones with dementia do not sleep. Surprisingly, when these caregivers subsequently keep a daily log of their loved one's sleep patterns, or have him or her wear a wrist activity-monitor that keeps an accurate record of their nighttime behavior, it turns out that many nights the person with dementia is sleeping fine![5] What is happening here? Why are some nights bad and others not? Is there something different about the person's sleeping environment or daytime routines or bedtime snack that might help explain the episodic nature of the sleep disturbances? Does the person always get up at the same time of night? Once out of bed, what does he or she do? What does the caregiver do to try to get the person back to bed, and what happens then?

Such questions are at the heart of creative behavioral problem solving. We must become like detectives, looking for clues in the immediate environment that may explain why a particular problem occurs sometimes, but not at other times. In the "ABCs of behavior change" model, caregivers are taught that "A" is the activator or triggering event that immediately precedes a problem behavior, "B" is the behavior of concern, and "C" is the immediate consequence or caregiver response to the behavior.[6] Dr. Linda Teri and her colleagues at the University of Washington (including myself) have used the ABC caregiver-training approach in the protocols of several research studies, successfully treating common dementia-related behavior problems, including depression, agitation, physical inactivity, and sleep disturbances.[7]

The ABC approach has six steps, which are illustrated in the Problem-Solving Example. This is the stage where having someone to brainstorm with is especially helpful; like Watson and Sherlock Holmes, all the best detectives work in pairs! You can see from this example how the aspects of creative problem solving that we discussed above can be applied in a structured way. Mrs. Q identifies a problem, gains new perspective on the problem by talking to her pastor and fellow parishioners, and tries some of their ideas.

PROBLEM-SOLVING EXAMPLE

1. *Identify the Behavior Problem*: Mr. Q makes suggestive comments and tries to hug and kiss the women he sees when he and his wife go to church.

2. *Gather Information*: This happened twice last week (Wednesday and Sunday).

3. *Identify Activators (Triggers) and Consequences*:
   a. *Activators*: Church acquaintances greeting Mr. and Mrs. Q when they arrive or are leaving church services. However, Mr. Q also sometimes acts this way with the waitresses when he and his wife are having breakfast at their favorite coffee shop.
   b. *Consequences*: Mrs. Q gets embarrassed and tells Mr. Q to cut it out; Mr. Q responds by becoming angry and raising his voice or repeating his comments even more

loudly; people in the congregation stare or avoid the couple.

4. *Brainstorm Solutions*:
   a. Mr. and Mrs. Q stop going to church.
   b. Mrs. Q goes to church alone, leaving her husband at home.
   c. Mr. and Mrs. Q switch to a different church where no one knows them, and it would not be so uncomfortable when Mr. Q acts strangely.
   d. Mr. and Mrs. Q come late for services and leave early so they are less likely to be greeted by fellow parishioners.
   e. Mrs. Q explains to people at the church about her husband's dementia, so they are more understanding.

5. *Select a Strategy*: Mrs. Q decided to talk to her pastor at the church about Mr. Q's dementia. The pastor said he had observed that Mr. Q was more likely to act this way when someone approached him with a welcoming hug. He suggested telling members of the congregation not to make physical contact with Mr. Q when greeting him. He also offered to help find someone to care for Mr. Q on Sunday mornings if Mrs. Q decided she wanted to leave her husband at home.

6. *Take Action/Evaluate Effectiveness*: Mrs. Q called fellow parishioners to explain about her husband's condition, and to pass on the pastor's suggestion about greeting Mr. Q. Everyone was very understanding, and agreed to help. Mrs. Q also started bringing her Bible to church and asked Mr. Q to carry if for her. As a result, his hands were full when they were coming and going, and he was less likely to engage in any inappropriate physical contacts with members of the congregation. (Note: This solution was not on Mrs. Q's original brainstorming list, but the idea was suggested to her by one of the women in the parish with whom she talked about her problem.)

Resolution

Mr. Q's inappropriate behaviors decreased. When they did happen, people ignored them while Mrs. Q redirected him to another topic. Mr. and Mrs. Q continued attending the parish where they had been church members for many years. Their fellow parishioners were a great source of social support, and Mr. Q very much enjoyed attending church functions and liturgies.

Several important points about creative problem solving can be made using this example. The first point is that it is important to be as specific as possible about the problem you want to change. The more clearly you can define a problem, the more likely it is that you will be able to carry out an effective course of action. For example, while you may "just want mother to be happy," this goal is too broad and unstructured. Using the ABCs also works best if you focus on problems that happen frequently and are easily observable. Doing this will make it easier for you to evaluate whether something you try makes the situation better or worse. Mrs. Q picked a problem that was happening every week, observed when and where it was occurring, and clearly articulated what she wanted to change. She was ready to brainstorm some solutions to try.

Mrs. Q's story provides a good example of how other people can be invaluable, both as assistants when you are brainstorming ideas, and as allies when you implement a behavioral plan. When you can identify potential triggers, or activators, for problem behaviors, that is a very powerful place to intervene. It is much easier to prevent a problem from getting started than it is to manage or eliminate the problem once it gets going. With the help of her pastor, Mrs. Q figured out that being hugged was a major trigger for her husband's behaviors. Asking people to change how they approached her husband helped eliminate that trigger. Another friend suggested giving Mr. Q a Bible to hold in his hands. Having something to hold made it more difficult to hug people and further decreased the likelihood that Mr. Q would engage in any inappropriate touching. Mrs. Q wondered if these same strategies would work in other settings. The next time they went to their favorite coffee shop, Mrs. Q called ahead and alerted her husband's favorite waitress and the restaurant owner to the plan. After the owner seated them, the waitress came over with the menus and casually greeted Mr. Q, without hugging him or being extra-friendly while she took their order, and then disappeared. There were no problems at the coffee shop that morning!

The consequences, or responses, to Mr. Q's behaviors also changed in this example. Instead of getting upset and avoiding Mr. Q, people now ignored his inappropriate behaviors, because they understood that he meant no harm and had no control over what he was saying or doing. As a result, Mrs. Q was less embarrassed and was better able to manage situations that did arise in a calm way. She found that quietly diverting Mr. Q's attention to some other person or object in the room was much more effective than her previous attempts to get him to stop doing or saying things by scolding or correcting him. Ultimately, the combination of eliminating the triggers, changing the consequences, and enlisting the help of other people in the problem solving process made it possible for Mr. and Mrs. Q to remain part of a valued community. As a result, they were less isolated and their quality of life was enhanced.

WHEN CREATIVE PROBLEM SOLVING DOES NOT WORK

Before closing this chapter, we should briefly consider those situations in which a creative behavioral problem solving approach is not the only, or even the best, one to use. When you are in the middle of an emergency or an acute crisis, behavioral interventions, even the most creative ones, are not your first line of defense. Emergency medical or pharmacological treatments may be necessary to keep you and your loved one safe. Later, after the dust settles, you will be able to take a look at what happened with your loved one and start to figure out some creative ways to try to keep it from happening again.

Jeb had always been a jealous husband. Since he had become demented, however, it was worse. He did not like his wife leaving the house, and he did not like her having visitors.

One day, Jeb got very angry when his wife asked him to do something. He began yelling at her and shoved her. Over the next several days, Jeb's behavior became more and more threatening until his wife began to seriously fear for her safety. She called 911 and Jeb was taken sedated to the hospital for evaluation. While there, it was discovered that he had an undiagnosed cancer. The doctor said Jeb was probably in considerable pain, which, added to his mental confusion, had led to his escalating violence.

In this example, Jeb was unable to communicate with his wife that something was physically very wrong with him, and his wife did not know what was happening. Her husband had never been an easy man to live with, and that had worsened in some respects since he had developed dementia. When Jeb's behavior began to deteriorate, his wife initially did not take it too seriously because she was accustomed to working around his moods. However, at some point she realized that it was no longer safe and called for help. This was the right thing to do. Every caregiver should have an escape plan, just in case an unexpected emergency arises. *Never* remain in a situation where you are fearful that your loved one could hurt you. If you find yourself feeling threatened, stay out of your loved one's reach until he or she is calmer; do not try to grab hold of the person or block their escape. Leave the house if necessary to prevent injury, and call for help.

It is also important to acknowledge that, even when there is no emergency, creative problem solving is not a magic bullet. There are occasions, to be sure, when the right trigger is found and a problem behavior is completely eliminated. More often, however, we are able to reduce the frequency, severity, and duration of behavior problems gradually over time. It takes time to find a different perspective on things, and it takes energy to brainstorm creative ideas and give them a try. If you are impatient, or are at the end of your rope and looking for a quick fix, this may not be the approach for you. Caregivers with high levels of stress from competing work or family responsibilities, or physical or mental health problems of their own, may feel less able to develop and follow through with a behavior-change plan. On the other hand, creative problem solving has no cost, no negative side effects, and can strengthen your sense of your own competence as a caregiver, while enriching your relationship with your loved one. Often, caregivers who begin to practice creative problem solving report that their own mood has improved, and that they feel less burdened and reactive to their loved one's problems, when they do occur. Give it a try, and see what happens for yourself!

SUMMARY

It is sometimes said that creativity is nothing more than an extra set of eyes. In this chapter, we explored how the process of creative problem solving can be broken down into steps all of us can learn. The most critical—and the most difficult—of these steps is the ability to look at your situation with an "extra set of eyes," to come up with new ways of doing things that may make the situation better. Sometimes, this extra set of eyes, or new perspective, comes from the people around you. Other times, it comes from systematically thinking about how your loved one's personal past could be influencing what is going on today, or by looking at the immediate context in which behavior problems occur, to see if you can find physical, environmental, or interpersonal causes. Just as it can be difficult to change old communication patterns or attitudes toward a loved one with dementia, eliminating triggers for behavior problems takes time and practice. It is important for you to be realistic and to set small, achievable goals that can be easily evaluated for their success. Creative problem solving is a skill that is worth taking the time to work at, however. No matter what stage of dementia your loved one is at, or what kinds of challenges you face, you will find that a little creativity, a fresh perspective, and the ability to brainstorm a list of ideas to try will give you the confidence that you can handle whatever comes your way.

EXERCISE

In the Problem-Solving Example, we outlined the story of Mr. and Mrs. Q to illustrate how one uses the ABCs for brainstorming in creative problem solving. Remember the steps? Here they are:

1. Identify the behavior problem. Be specific! Pick a behavior that you can see and count.

2. Gather information. When and where does the problem occur? Who is around when it happens?

3. Look for possible activators (these are the "triggers," or what happens immediately before the problem) and consequences (this is what happens immediately after the problem, often what you or other people do in response to its occurrence). Focus on activators and consequences in the environment that you can see and modify.

4. Brainstorm a list of ideas of what you could do to change any activators or consequences. Remember that two heads are better than one for helping you generate new ideas. At this stage, do not evaluate your ideas. Just get as many down on paper as possible. The only rules are that your ideas should focus on what *you* (not your loved one) can change or do differently, and that the options should be loving and respectful. Don't argue!

5. Take action. Pick something on your list and give it a try. It is okay to do more than one thing on the list, but keep it simple. Consistency is important, and if you are trying to do too much at once, you will have a hard time sticking with the plan.

6. Evaluate what happened. See what happens over the next week or two. Does the problem get better or worse?

Now, pick one problem that you have been having in caring for your loved one. Using these steps and the Problem-Solving Example as your guide, on a separate piece of paper, go through the ABCs and generate a creative problem-solving plan. What is the activator or trigger? What is the Behavior that concerns you? What has been the Consequence or your response to that Behavior?

Take your time. Talk with family and friends to get their perspectives on what might be triggering the problem or what might be making things better or worse. Do not worry if some of your ideas seem silly or overly simplistic. Then try one. Just do something—*anything*—differently and see what happens.

Chapter 6

E: ENJOY THE MOMENT ◆

Talk to any resilient caregiver, and you will be reminded that the day-to-day life with someone who has dementia is not always difficult or tragic. Often, if you are paying attention, there are moments of intimacy, satisfaction, or even hilarity that the two of you share. This was one episode that Lois recalled:

> "LOIS!!!!!" Jeff's urgent cry carried through the window to the bedroom where Lois was resting. Lois jumped up, ran down the stairs, and out the back door, expecting to find Jeff on the ground, injured in some way. Instead, he was standing in front of a large rose bush covered with brilliant scarlet blooms. As Lois rushed over, furious and perplexed over what was the big emergency, Jeff turned to her with a brilliant smile and pointed to a large bud about to open. "Isn't it beautiful?" he asked. "I wanted you to be the first to see it."

At that instant, Lois was torn between wanting to kill her husband of fifty-plus years for scaring her half to death, and wanting to embrace him with tenderness for the gentle insight into his dementia that she had just been given. Persons with dementia live purely in the moment. In a negative sense, this leads to great "selfishness." They forget to say "thank you," and gradually lose the ability to understand and appreciate the degree to which other people are extending themselves. It would have never occurred to Jeff that he might alarm his wife with his frantic hollering. On the other hand, this tendency to live in the moment provides observant caregivers with an intimate snapshot into their loved one's inner experiences. Unlike most of us who wear a public persona that conceals our deepest longings, fears, and desires, people with dementia wear their true selves on their sleeves. When they are happy, they smile and are calm. When they are frightened, they may pace about or strike out in an effort to escape. When they are hot, they may take off their clothes, oblivious to the fact that they are in a fancy restaurant. This uncensored openness can create many difficult moments, of course, but it also gives the caregiver a true glimpse into the soul of someone they love.

In this chapter, we will talk about three ways to enjoy the moment that are not only possible, but also, indeed, part and parcel of providing resilient care for someone with dementia. First, you will learn how to develop a repertoire of pleasant events that make life more enjoyable for your loved one with dementia and for yourself, which will in turn help both of you achieve better moods and also reduce your loved one's risk for developing many dementia-related behavior problems. Second, by learning to notice the daily "uplifts" and satisfactions you experience from providing care, and by seeing how these satisfactions are grounded in the values you hold and bring to caregiving, you will find new meaning in your role and become more resilient in handling your daily challenges and difficulties. Finally, allowing yourself to relax into those moments of laughter when unexpected, endearing, or just plain funny things happen to you and your loved one will help you gain perspective in a healthy way.

ENJOYING PLEASANT ACTIVITIES TOGETHER

What do you enjoy doing? Chances are that if someone asked you this question, you would have a variety of answers that are on a continuum of very simple to very complicated or expensive. You might enjoy walking with friends at dawn, watching a favorite TV program, playing with your dog, going to the opera, or traveling to exotic places around the world. Many things that we enjoy have a physical or a sensory quality: hugging a child, soaking in a warm bath, petting a purring cat in the lap, or smelling garlic and butter sautéing in the kitchen. Others involve practiced skills: playing bridge with friends, swimming in an open-water race, or cultivating the perfect rose garden.

When a person develops dementia, their interests and abilities change. In some cases, they withdraw themselves from previously enjoyed activities. For example, the expert bridge player may stop joining the usual weekly game because she is embarrassed that she can no longer play a good hand. In some other cases, the people around them determine what activities persons with dementia continue to do. The demented husband may still want to work in his woodshop, building birdhouses, but his wife worries about his safety using power tools. In still other cases, it is not obvious why our loved ones no longer want to do things that always brought them pleasure, like attending Sunday dinners with the kids, or arranging bouquets of flowers from the garden. It appears that they are still capable of doing these things, but they just seem to have lost interest. That was what happened to Sam.

Sam was a runner. He had pictures of himself running in marathons all over the country, long before running was a popular thing to do. Rain or shine, he ran seven miles to and from work every day of his long career as a local mechanic. He took his kids, and then his grandkids and great-grandkids, out running for every charitable event that came along. Even now, in his early eighties, Sam had the long, lean look of a man who could jog around the retirement community without breaking a sweat. Since he had been diagnosed with dementia, however, Sam had stopped running. In fact, he no longer would even walk with his wife or other family members when they came to visit. He would say, "I just don't feel like it right now," or "Maybe later, I'm busy," or "It's too cold (or hot) outside today," or "I'm too tired." Running had been the greatest love of Sam's life, but now he was done with it.

Sam not only had memory loss, but was also depressed. His wife became worried about this sudden, severe apathy and took him to their family doctor. The doctor explained that although loss of interest and withdrawal from activities can be directly caused by dementia, these symptoms may also indicate that a person is suffering from a treatable mood disorder. She suggested that they try placing Sam on an antidepressant medication. A couple of months later, Sam resumed his morning walks with his wife. He never again initiated them, and sometimes when she would ask, Sam would still refuse with one of his standard excuses. His wife, however, learned that if she told Sam it was time for their walk, rather than asking him whether or not he wanted to go, he was more likely to agree, and he always seemed to enjoy it once they got going.

Sam was lucky. Sam's family did not take "no" for an answer or give up on him. They no longer expected (or wanted) him to go on long, solitary jogs or to run in marathons. However, they recognized that giving up all the physical activity that he always loved so much was not good for Sam, not while he was still so healthy and there were people who enjoyed going out with him. Sam could no longer do many of the things he had done in the past, but there were still things—like walking in the park with his family—that he was capable of and that brought him pleasure. Sam had to give up some of what he liked doing, but not everything.

This is true for all of us, whether or not we have dementia. Sometimes, what we do for pleasure changes because we discover something new to be interested in. Sometimes, changes happen because our health, finances, or circumstances alter what we can do for fun. Some changes happen precipitously, or are unwelcome; some happen gradually and we cannot wait for them to get here. The only thing that is constant is that everyone needs to have things in their life that bring them happiness and joy. In this respect, your loved one with dementia is no different from you or from anyone else. What a liberating thought! Dr. Steven Albert, a geriatric psychologist at Columbia University interested in the quality of life for sufferers of Alzheimer's disease, has said that the one thing persons with dementia retain, no matter how advanced their disease, is the ability to know what (or whom) they like.[1] In some cases, discovering what brings pleasure to a loved one with dementia—and giving it to them—can make all the difference.

Millie's mom, Madeline, lived in another state. Madeline was diagnosed with vascular dementia. When Madeline's husband died, Millie moved Madeline to a nursing home in her parents' small hometown. The move was difficult. Madeline was confused and upset, and few of her old friends and neighbors came to visit. Millie was tormented with guilt. To make matters worse, Madeline's dementia seemed to be "getting better"; the staff reported that Madeline was doing things for herself that Millie had thought were beyond her. Millie was terrified that her mother had been misdiagnosed with dementia and should never have been moved to a nursing home. Then, during one visit, Millie discovered what was going on. The home had a nurse's aide who had developed a particular fondness for Madeline and taken her "under her wing." The aide combed Madeline's hair, sang to her, and complimented her sweet smile, which showed up on Madeline's face more and more often. Millie realized that her mother had been very depressed as well as demented; the aide's kindness had led to such improvements in her mood that Madeline could now function better despite her cognitive limitations. Millie was able to put her mind at ease, knowing that her mom was thriving in her new home.

Unlike Sam, Madeline's depression was never diagnosed or treated by a physician; nevertheless, through the kindness and loving attention of another human being, her mood and function improved. Antidepressant medication therapies are very helpful for some people, but these medications can be costly and ineffective, and can also cause intolerable side effects. Pleasant events, on the other hand, can be free, readily available, and pose no risk to the recipient! Drs. Linda Teri and Rebecca Logsdon at the University of Washington were the first researchers to write about and investigate the relationship between depression in Alzheimer's disease (AD) and pleasant events. In one study, depressed persons with AD and their family caregivers were assigned to one of four groups—two active treatment and two control. In one of the active treatment groups, caregivers were taught to use the ABC approach, described in Chapter 5, in combination with increasing patient participation in pleasant events.[2] Over nine sessions, therapists helped caregivers to identify triggers for depressive episodes, to respond to these episodes more effectively using strategies such as reassurance and distraction, and to find activities that the person with dementia was capable of doing, and could enjoy on a regular basis. The ABC Pleasant Event treatment significantly reduced symptoms of depression in the persons with dementia at the two-month follow-up, and improvements were sustained four months later. Significantly, caregiver depression levels also improved, even though the intervention was not designed to target caregiver depression or anxiety.

Since this pioneering work was done, pleasant activities have been shown to improve the nighttime sleep patterns of institutionalized persons with dementia, and have been used as a means of enhancing the quality of life for in-home and institutionalized older adults.[3] Complementary therapies based on pleasurable or recreational experiences, such as animal-assisted therapy, music, movement, or art therapy, aromatherapy, and massage have also been reported to help improve the mood and behavior of cognitively impaired individuals. Although these reports are most often based on small numbers of subjects and uncontrolled research circumstances, they do point to the increasing recognition of the value of enhancing enjoyability of life for persons with dementia.

Many caregivers I talk to about this idea find it very difficult to figure out what pleasant activities that their loved one is capable of doing, will enjoy, and will agree to try. To assist caregivers in brainstorming ideas for pleasant activities, Drs. Teri and Logsdon developed a checklist of twenty activities that are simple and pleasurable for persons with dementia. Items on this checklist, the Pleasant Events Schedule for Alzheimer's Disease (PES-AD), are rated both in terms of how enjoyable the demented individual finds them to be, and how frequently they have done each activity in the past month.[4] (A copy of this checklist is provided at the end of this chapter.) This combination approach to thinking about what you and your loved one enjoy can be very helpful in a couple of ways. First, if there are things that he or she enjoys doing but is not doing regularly now, you might consider whether those activities, or some simplified variant of them, could be added back into the routine. Getting Sam walking every day was an example of this approach. Alternatively, if there are activities that have never been a source of pleasure, such as watching TV or window-shopping at the mall, these might not be good ones to ask your loved one to take up now, no matter how distracting or enjoyable they may be for you. If, on reflection, you discover that for reasons of convenience or lack of any better ideas, you have inadvertently allowed your loved one to slip into a pattern of spending time doing things that he or she never much cared for, now is the time to put on your thinking hat and see if you can come up with alternative ideas. One resilient caregiver discovered that doing so made life a little easier for both herself and her demented mom.

Mrs. M kept asking her daughter, Zoe, "What should I do?" Zoe would tell her mom to just sit down and relax, she would take care of everything. Ten minutes later, her mom would be back, asking, "What should I do?" The problem was that Zoe did not actually want her mom to do anything, because she needed continual supervision, and usually whatever Mrs. M did had to be done over again anyway. It was easier for Zoe just to do it herself. On the other hand, there were days when Zoe thought that if she heard Mrs. M say "What should I do?" one more time, she would scream. One day, Zoe and her sister were having coffee and they got to reminiscing about what an active woman Mrs. M had always been. With seven kids and a menagerie of pets around the house, she never had a minute to herself except when she was able to go off to the back room and work on the mountain of laundry that always needed ironing. Laughing about how that was probably the reason Mrs. M always loved ironing, Zoe suddenly realized that her mom was accustomed to neither being waited upon nor sitting alone inactive in a quiet house. No wonder she was always looking for something to do! In a flash of inspiration, Zoe got out an old iron and cut off the cord. The next time her mom wandered over looking for something to do, Zoe set up the ironing board and handed Mrs. M the old iron and a pile of towels, asking if she would like to help. It became their regular routine that while Zoe prepared dinner at night, Mrs. M would stand nearby and happily "iron" those towels.

Perhaps you are thinking to yourself, "This is going to be a lot of work!" The good news is that it does not necessarily have to be. Strategies for increasing pleasant events can be very simple; almost every encounter with a demented individual has the potential to be enjoyable for both parties.[5] As we saw with Madeline, being complimented, touched in a loving way, and sung to was all she needed to blossom. Pleasant events can be as complicated as a planned outing to an exotic place, or as simple as holding hands on a porch swing in a summer breeze. Creativity is all you need, plus a long list of options so that the pleasant events do not get boring or mechanical for either one of you. You want to have plenty of alternatives to try at different times and places. Pleasant events are often variations of things that the person enjoyed in the past. The dressmaker may still derive great pleasure from folding and handling fabric samples that are now boxed up in the sewing room. The retired business executive may enjoy looking at the *Wall Street Journal* every morning, even though he no longer has the capacity to understand or remember the information. The man who enjoyed building fine furniture in the past may still get great pleasure from sanding the front of an old table with a sheet of sandpaper. The woman who kept a spotless house may happily sweep the floor or dust the furniture. The point is not whether the job is well done. You are not giving your loved one chores to ease your work load. You are helping him or her find a sense of dignity, satisfaction, usefulness, or pleasure. Even if your loved one cannot articulate how he or she feels, it will make a difference. Increasing pleasant activities is good medicine for the both of you.

ENJOYING THE SATISFACTIONS IN CAREGIVING

A caregiver once told me that taking care of his wife reminded him of an old Zen belief that the most lowly chores in life are really the most important. It does seem to be the case that caregivers who are able to find value in the challenges they face are often the same ones whom I consider resilient. This is what Jennifer had to say:

> I am a baby boomer, the ultimate child of the 1960s. I don't think it's any accident that Alzheimer's disease has come to visit my generation with such a vengeance. Alzheimer's is the perfect complement to the "me" generation. It's an opportunity to experience taking care of someone who has lost all the things that we care the most about—autonomy, intelligence, youth. It makes you realize that you have to live life well right now, because you can't count on having it your way in the future. It also reminds you that "feeling good" isn't really so important. Pleasure comes and goes, but in the big picture, caring for a person with Alzheimer's is heartwarming and enriching, even if it's not always "fun." I've learned things about my dad I would have never gotten to know if I hadn't done this. It's payback for everything that man did for me over the years.

The role of caregiver is inherently a mixture of good and bad. The same activities that increase your satisfaction with helping your loved one often also increase your stress and burden.[6] Being able to see the satisfaction that comes with your daily responsibilities can help tip the balance toward resilient caregiving. There is a growing body of research that shows that dementia caregivers like Jennifer, who are able to identify "uplifts" in their daily activities—that is, things that make them feel good, joyful, glad, or satisfied—are better able to respond to their daily challenges and maintain their physical and mental health. But how do you do that? How can you wake up and pay attention to the gift as well as the cost of being a dementia caregiver? The ways that resilient caregivers accomplish this, and the form it takes, vary tremendously, but there seem to be three common threads that make it possible: building on the relationship you have with your loved one, leaning on spiritual or existential beliefs, and practicing gratitude.

Caregiving Relationships

Dr. Mike Nolan and his colleagues at the University of Sheffield have noted that many health-care providers and researchers tend to focus on either the needs of the person with dementia or on the needs of the caregiver. But that is not all there is to the story. If you really want to understand what a caregiving situation is like, you have to think about the dementia "triad": the person with dementia, the caregiver, *and* the *relationship* between them, with all its rich history and complexity.[7] As we saw in earlier chapters, relationships influence our communication patterns with persons with dementia, as well as our ability to accept their moods and behavior. So, too, relationships are at the heart of learning to enjoy the positive aspects of being a caregiver.

In some cases, historical relationship is the key. The grandson who always admired his grandmother's spirit and humor is likely to see glimpses of these qualities in her actions after she becomes demented, and to appreciate these glimpses because they remind him of the person his grandmother has been to him all his life. Spousal relationships often have a long history of loving and relating to one another in quiet, intimate ways. Having dementia does not necessarily undermine such long-standing closeness. One study even showed that husbands with dementia were actually *more* likely to engage in nonverbal, rapport-building interactions with their caregiving wives during structured tasks than their nondemented counterparts.[8] Think about this with your loved one. What qualities can you see now that you loved or admired about him or her in the past? Can you recognize that they are a reminder of the person your loved one still is, despite his or her dementing illness?

In other cases, it is in the current relationship where uplifts are found. Caregivers may experience great satisfaction in being able to help those they love, or, like Jennifer, may feel like they actually know and understand their loved ones better because of the illness, and so are closer to them now than in the past. Dementia sometimes takes the edge off a demanding personality and makes that person easier to get along with now than when he or she was younger. This was the case with Janet.

> Janet had never been an easy person to make friends with. She was too critical and too shy to be an easy companion for others. So it was surprising when, after Janet moved to an assisted-living facility, she became such fast friends with Margo, who lived in the same wing and also had memory problems. As far as Janet's daughter could tell, the two were always together. Constant company for one another, they would talk and talk and talk. One day, Janet's daughter and son-in-law came by to help with the laundry and tidy up the apartment. The four were walking down the hallway—Janet, Margo, and Janet's daughter and son-in-law—talking about something Janet had done as a younger woman. All of a sudden, Margo stopped, turned around, and said, "There's just one thing I want to know." The others looked at her and nodded, "Yes, what is it?" "I just want to know," Margo said, "Who's Janet?" Janet's family roared with laughter but were also touched. Margo had dementia, too, of course, and could not remember her new best friend's name. But Margo also did not recognize the irritable and demanding Janet in the children's stories to be the same person who meant so much to her now.

It was not only Margo and Janet's family who benefited from Janet's softening personality as she became more demented. For the first time in her life, Janet found herself unexpectedly enveloped in new relationships that accepted her as she was, without expectations or anxieties based upon her past foibles and mistakes, and forgave her readily (even forgot!) when she made those same mistakes today. In relating this story, Janet's daughter expressed amazement that such a debilitating condition as Alzheimer's disease could nevertheless have such generative, community-building aspects to it. She said, "My—and my mom's—worlds became so much bigger than they would have been if she had just grown old and died in her own home."

Spirituality

Many caregivers talk about finding meaning in their role in the context of their religious or existential beliefs. Certainly, believers in traditional religious cultures such as Judaism, Christianity, Islam, or Buddhism can find scriptural and service traditions that promote selflessness, generosity, and acceptance of personal suffering. In Chapter 3, I described a caregiver, Madge, who found acceptance and meaning in her role from her experiences and reflections on the philosophy of Alcoholics Anonymous. Carol Farran, a researcher at Rush University, has drawn from the existential writings of Victor Frankl to study how caregivers find meaning through both their positive and negative experiences of caring for a person with dementia.[9] Common spiritual themes reported by caregivers include: (1) taking charge by reaching out to family, friends, and church communities for inspiration and support; (2) adjustment/coping, which includes the use of prayer for strength and increased understanding; and (3) making sense of the situation, which may involve counting one's blessings, trusting in a higher power, or seeing one's caregiving experiences as being part of a larger plan.[10]

These themes ring true in light of many stories I have heard from caregivers over the years. For example, Melody described her caregiving situation in this way:

I was one of six kids in a solidly Catholic family. When mom was diagnosed with Alzheimer's disease, I knew I would be the one who would take care of her. She lives with us now. We have five kids ourselves and so it is always a commotion—someone has lost their homework, someone needs a sandwich before soccer practice, mom is upset because she can't find her favorite shirt that I finally put in the laundry. Still, it is a blessing, really. I feel so privileged to be taking care of her after all that she and dad did to take care of us. I take mom with me to the kids' events and to church. We sit in the back so that if we have to leave early it won't be disruptive, but people understand and everyone is so nice. And what's great is that when people are nice to mom, she just gives it right back. She may not know who they are any more, but when people have a smile and a kind voice, she acts like they are her best friends. I am lucky to have mom, and so glad she taught me the importance of loving and taking care of other people.

Gratitude

Melody was a woman who strongly identified with her Catholic faith. For her, taking care of mom was an extension of the values her parents had taught her while growing up, and a reflection of the person she wanted to be. From my point of view, however, one of the particularly important defining characteristics of Melody was her sense of gratitude. Melody genuinely appreciated the fact that her parents had provided for her and her siblings, and wanted to "pass it on." Her "attitude of gratitude" permeated every aspect of her mother's care.

I am aware of no research studies that have examined the construct of gratitude in dementia caregivers. On one hand, it seems like an anomalous idea. What is there to be grateful about when you are caring for someone with Alzheimer's disease? But in fact, many caregivers I talk with speak of gratitude. Unlike Melody, they are not always grateful to be taking care of someone who has dementia, to be sure. But caregivers find other things to be grateful for: for their relative physical health or that of their loved ones, for family and friends who help when they can, for a house that is paid off, for a nearby day-care center with a reasonable sliding pay scale, or for the absence of behavioral problems in their loved ones that are so frightening in other people. When you start to look, there is always something to be grateful for; there is always someone who is having a more difficult time than yourself. A friend who works with persons who have dementia told me Jack's story.

Eileen was able to stay at home, despite her advanced dementia, because her husband Jack was committed to her total care. He told me that the highlight of his day came in the evening when she was finally calm, clean, fed, and relaxed. Although Eileen rarely spoke, they watched *Wheel of Fortune* every night, sitting in front of the TV and holding hands. When I asked Jack how he was able to do so much, he replied, "She's still my sweetheart." Jack was grateful to still have Eileen with him, and at the end of every day, that was all that really mattered.

Gratitude is a powerful ally that resilient caregivers can call upon. Entire systems of psychotherapy have been built around teaching individuals to reflect upon the things in their lives for which they should be grateful.[11] It is easy to remember present or past hurts and troubles when we are in the midst of a difficult situation. It may be harder to focus on how much we owe the many persons who have helped and supported us over our lifetime. In the world of caregivers, gratitude is the yeast that helps many people grow bigger than they ever thought they could be. Resilient caregivers are grateful when their loved one takes the morning medication without complaint, grateful when they get an unexpected afternoon nap, and grateful for that beautiful rose they would have overlooked if it had not been pointed out to them. What are you grateful for?

ENJOYING HUMOR TOGETHER

One of the first poems I memorized as a little girl was *Solitude*, by Ella Wheeler Wilcox, with its famous opening lines: "Laugh, and the world laughs with you; / Weep, and you weep alone. / For the sad old earth must borrow it's mirth, / But has trouble enough of it's own."[12] A caregiver friend recently reminded me of these lines as she talked about the ways that humor enriched her experiences of caring for her demented mother. She shared this story of her mother.

Hilde had grown up in the "old country" and still had extended family living in Germany and Austria. One of Hilde's nephews lived nearby and came often to visit Hilde. Whenever he would stop by, Hilde would ask, "Where is your mother these days?" The nephew would reply, "Germany," and immediately Hilde would launch into a loud, clear recitation of Heinrich Heine's poem *Lorelei* ("Ich weib nicht, was soll es bedeuten...."). There was no stopping her until the entire poem was finished, and Hilde was beaming with pleasure over her recitation. For the nephew—and any other visitors who happened to be there at the time—it became a predictable, and hilarious, routine. Hilde loved it that everyone seemed to enjoy her poetry so much.

For my friend, the ability to laugh at things that would happen with her mom was not only a way of releasing tension for herself, but it also had a positive, infectious effect. When my friend laughed, her mother saw a jolly person and would get into a good mood! My friend's mom never seemed to mind (or even notice) that it was something she had said or done that caused the laughter. All that mattered was there was a spirit of happiness in the air that brought them closer for a moment.

The publication of Norman Cousins' 1979 book, *Anatomy of an Illness as Perceived by the Patient*, popularized the idea that laughter can cure disease.[13] Since that time, the healing power of humor and laughter has gained considerable attention in the medical literature as well as in the popular caregiving press. Although many claims about laughter and health have no research basis, there is good evidence that humor plays an important role in patient–health-care provider communication and in patient care. It is certainly the case that humor, when used appropriately, relieves stress, puts people at ease, and, as in the case below, makes it possible to forget, at least for a little while, whatever is bothering you.

Jim kept getting up at night, usually around 2 a.m. His wife, Pat, would get up and eventually get him back to bed, only to then lie awake herself for several hours before she would finally drift off to a nonrestorative sleep. One night, Jim got up and Pat followed him into the kitchen. "Jim!" she cried, "what are you doing?" Her husband, who had been a career naval officer at sea for many years, turned and replied, "I'm on watch." Pat snapped, "That's ridiculous—now go to bed!" Looking puzzled, Jim asked, "Who are you?" Pat promptly retorted, "Listen sailor! It doesn't matter who I am. I outrank you! Now go to bed!" When Jim meekly turned around and headed back to the bedroom, Pat collapsed in a kitchen chair and laughed silently until tears rolled down her cheeks.

When Pat told me this story, we both laughed again. For Pat, being able to laugh at what had become a very difficult situation for her was a survival technique. Her amusement at Jim's obedient response to her spontaneous command also helped her put his nighttime activities in perspective. She now realized that Jim's wandering was neither "crazy" nor a deliberate attempt to annoy her. He had simply reverted back to a sleep/wake activity pattern that had been normal for many years in his younger life. Having this perspective allowed her to consider alternative strategies for helping Jim get back into sync with the rest of the world. Her laughter helped her get unstuck and be able to shift into a more effective problem-solving mode.

Laughter is a valuable tool for caregivers in learning not to take themselves too seriously. I remember meeting with one couple in my clinic. When I spoke privately with the husband, he was so apologetic—in his rush to get out the door that morning, he had inadvertently put his wife's sweater on inside out and had not noticed until they were sitting in the clinic waiting room right before their appointment. For this kind gentleman, the main point was that I should not think badly of his wife, since it was his fault, not hers, that she had come in so inappropriately attired. For me, however, it was an opportunity to try to gently help the man make contact with how hard his life had become as he struggled to cover up his wife's memory problems so that no one else would see them. As we chuckled together about his puzzlement regarding things like brassieres and panty hose, the husband began to describe his reticence and grief over having to tell his children about their mother's dementia diagnosis. It was only after he was able to let down his guard and defensive protectiveness of his beloved wife's image that he could admit how difficult it had been caring for her all alone. Humor was the gate that allowed him to ask for help.

Finally, resilient caregivers have told me that one of the most valuable things about humor in dementia care is that it creates and sustains relationships, both with the loved one who has dementia, and with other people who become part of your caregiving world. As the disease progresses, and the person with dementia becomes increasingly forgetful, caregivers become a social lifeline for their loved ones. The process of introducing and reintroducing people in the neighborhood or retirement community over and over often leads to many chuckles, and creates an opportunity for the caregiver to get to know well a world of people that he or she barely knew before. Yolanda told this story:

> When I was taking care of my father, I met another woman through a support group who was about my age and who also had her dad living at home with her. We hit it off, and used to get together whenever we could, maybe once a month. We'd go to one another's house, and take our fathers along. The four of us would sit around in the living room, maybe with a football game on the TV. She and I would talk nonstop about our families and lives and laugh about everything. Most of the time, our dads would just sit there, not watching TV or saying much, not even always awake. But they seemed to like it anyway. When my girlfriend and I would get to giggling, the men would kind of sit up, and grin. I don't think they had a clue most of the time as to what we were talking about, but just sitting around together, all four of us, seemed so *normal* and fun. Nothing else really mattered.

The scenario that Yolanda described was one in which both the caregivers and their fathers were able to simply enjoy being together on a regular basis. Although they never said so, the men seemed to appreciate being included in a family activity that was joyful and that placed no performance demands upon them. Their daughters were able to spend time with another person who understood completely what it was like to be juggling the roles of wife, mother, and dementia caregiver. They never had to worry about someone else being available to take care of their dad, nor be concerned about what the other would think if one of the men did something unusual during the visit. It was such a relief to be able to laugh and be silly for a while. These monthly visits brought the fathers and daughters closer together and deepened the women's blossoming friendship. In Yolanda's case, the friendship that was nurtured during these monthly visits has survived many years beyond the deaths of both men.

SUMMARY

To the outside observer, it may seem impossible that anyone caring for someone with dementia could ever "enjoy the moment." However, if you are a caregiver, you can come to see things differently. Caring for a loved one with dementia is challenging and sometimes unpleasant, but it can also be tender, satisfying, and downright funny. Resilient caregivers look for opportunities to participate in enjoyable activities with their loved ones. Having fun more often can not only bring both of you pleasure, but can also reduce the boredom and many dementia-related mood or behavior problems in the person for whom you are caring. Resilient caregivers learn to look for the uplifts and satisfaction in their role, whether these come from interpersonal relationships (including the one you share with your loved one), from your spiritual or philosophical belief systems, or from gratitude at having a half-full glass rather than one that is half-empty. Enjoying the moment also, at times, comes from the funny and poignant moment that you share with your loved one. It is okay to laugh when he or she does something that tickles your funny bone! It is also okay to laugh at yourself when things do not go right. It will be easier to ask for the help that you need to nurture yourself if you can take your job a little less seriously. Doing so will allow you to reach out to friends, family members, health-care professionals, and other caregivers who want to help.

◆ EXERCISE

This exercise is a series of questions designed to get you thinking about pleasant activities and the satisfaction that you can find caring for your loved one.

Name three things that your loved one used to do for fun. Then name three things that *you* used to do for fun (either individually or together).

_____

_____

_____

How often have either of you done any of these things in the past month? If you have done any or all of them frequently (i.e., more than once a week), congratulations! You are on the right track. If you have not done any of these things, why?

_____

_____

_____

If you and your loved one are already participating in many activities that bring both of you pleasure, your challenge is to keep it up. Can you think of obstacles that may come along that will prevent you from continuing to do these things? How will you deal with these obstacles? (The goal is not to keep you always doing the same things, but to ensure that both you and your loved one continue to have regular experiences in your life that bring you happiness and satisfaction.)

_____

_____

_____

If you and your loved one are not doing many activities that bring you pleasure, try looking at the Pleasant Events Schedule at the end of this chapter (Table 4) to see if it can help you think of activities that you could try during the upcoming week. Try also considering the following possibilities.

What can you do that will stimulate your loved one's senses? Petting a cat, giving a hug, kneading dough, stroking a soft blanket, having one's hair brushed or hand cream applied, watching fish in a tank or people in the mall, listening to a tape of ocean sounds or a big band CD, and baking (and tasting) cookies are all examples of activities that awaken one's pleasurable senses of touch, sight, hearing, smell, and taste.

What kind of work or hobbies did your loved one do that he or she enjoyed? Are there variants of household, recreational, or community

TABLE 4. Pleasant Events Schedule for Alzheimer's Disease Patients (Family Version)

This schedule contains a list of events or activities that people sometimes enjoy. It is designed to find out about things your relative has enjoyed during the past month. Please rate each item twice. The first time, rate each item on how many times it happened in the past month (frequency); the second time, rate each event on how much your relative enjoyed the activity.

	Frequency			Enjoyability		
	Not At All	*1–6 Times*	*7 or More Times*	*Not At All*	*Some-what*	*A Great Deal*

Activity

 1. Being outside
 2. Shopping, buying things
 3. Reading or listening to stories, magazines, newspapers
 4. Listening to music
 5. Watching TV
 6. Laughing
 7. Having meals with friends or family
 8. Making or eating snacks
 9. Helping around the house
10. Being with family
11. Wearing favorite clothes
12. Listening to the sounds of nature (birdsong, wind, surf)
13. Getting/sending letters, cards
14. Going on outings (to the park, a picnic, etc.)
15. Having coffee, tea, etc., with friends
16. Being complimented
17. Exercising (walking, dancing, etc.)
18. Going for a ride in the car
19. Grooming (wearing makeup, shaving, having hair cut)
20. Recalling and discussing past events

activities that would bring your loved one pleasure? Washing windows, trimming the laurel bush, sweeping floors, dusting, raking leaves, sorting drawers of clothes or different sizes of screws and bolts, and accompanying you on neighborhood errands may all be enjoyable for a person with dementia who was active and service oriented in his or her younger years. Try offering something—anything—for your loved one to do. Persons with dementia often surprise us by enjoying activities we would never have expected them to like.

Was your loved one a "people person" in his or her younger days? Spending time with persons from a variety of age groups—infants to school-age kids, young adults to other seniors, family members or fellow attendees at the local adult day-care center—can all be pleasurable for your loved one. It may be that social activities need to be scaled down in size; a visit from one or two is often better than an entire family reunion. It may also be helpful to remember that your loved one may not be concerned about all the things you are concerned about, such as what clothes to wear, whether or not the house is clean, or how anyone's hair looks. The companionship is what counts.

Finally, what can you do as part of your relationship with your loved one that will make his or her day a little brighter? Every encounter with your loved one is an opportunity to be P.O.L.I.T.E. (Refer back to Table 2 on p. 42 if you have forgotten these communication techniques.) The best pleasant events are often brief and spontaneous. Your smile, your tone of voice, your touch, your laughter, and your consistency are all pleasant events for someone with dementia. Equally important, they are much-needed pleasant events for you as well. Try it, and see what happens.

Section III

THE PROMISE:

You Can Do It!

Throughout this book, we have been talking about a handful of practical strategies that can help you to be more resilient as you face the ups and downs of caring for a loved one with dementia. Each of the D.A.N.C.E. principles—**D**on't argue, **A**ccept the disease, **N**urture your physical and emotional health, use **C**reative problem solving, and **E**njoy the moment with your loved one—are designed to be flexible guidelines, not a rigid prescription of behaviors, for you to follow. There is no single road to successful caregiving, no one "right way." It is like good cooking: you have to experiment, trust your instincts, and learn from your mistakes. If you can experiment with the ideas I have given you here, make them your own, and improve on them, then this book will have done its job well.[1]

Some of you reading this book may feel that although in theory the D.A.N.C.E. principles seem reasonable, in practice they are just too much to take on. If it seems that way to you, do not be discouraged. You are not alone. Any kind of change takes time, and we often spend a long period thinking what we want to do before we actually give it a try.[2] Change is particularly unsettling when you cannot predict for certain what will happen as a result of all your efforts. Learning skills to become a more resilient caregiver is like getting into your car and heading on a road trip where you know the general direction but not the precise route. There will be many twists and turns, surprises and detours along the way, places of great beauty, and places you will feel like you cannot get past quick enough. As a dementia caregiver, you cannot control everything about the path on which you are traveling, but the D.A.N.C.E. principles will help you keep from getting lost or crashing along the way. The trick is not to give up before you begin.

Three secrets will help you to not become overwhelmed and give up on your quest to become a more resilient caregiver. First, you have to remember why you are caring for your loved one in the first place. We have talked throughout this book about values—both the personal values that give meaning to your caregiver role, and the value that your loved one has as a human being, regardless of how dementia has changed him or her. Why are you a caregiver? Of all the people in your loved one's life, why are you the one who is there to help him or her? Is it to give back to someone who has given so much to you in the past? Is it because your loved one needs help, and you are a person who believes that helping others is important? Are you drawing upon a personal faith, or a philosophy that gives you strength? Can you in your heart make contact with the real person that you are caring for—see not just his or her symptoms of dementia, but the man or woman behind them whom you love and who has loved you in return? Staying in contact with your values and the things your loved one can still teach you will help you keep from becoming overwhelmed with the everyday hassles of caregiving. Your values, those things that give your caregiving meaning and purpose, are like the North Star of dementia care, helping you to see where you are heading, instead of only seeing the boulders you have to climb over along the way. Kerry described it to me like this:

> The event that had the most impact on me came when I visited my elderly father in the nursing home, twelve years ago. I was on my way down to the dementia unit. When the elevator doors opened, I was staring at the wall in front of me, which had huge letters reading, "HONOR THY FATHER AND THY MOTHER." It suddenly hit me what those words meant. Not just for my own parents, but for all of the parents I was

about to go inside to see. I knew whatever I took out of there would be more than I brought in. My parents are long gone, but I now have an opportunity to honor my parents by caring for my in-laws. It is an honor to have them in our home.

The second secret to staying on the path to resilience is to remember that your goal is not perfection. When you are learning something that is new and difficult, it is so easy to get angry and disappointed when things do not go as well as you had hoped! Unfortunately, if you focus too hard on your mistakes or inadequacies, you may become discouraged and give up. You will never reach a point where you always avoid arguments, always nurture yourself the way you should, or always come up with a creative solution to whatever troublesome problem comes your way. Resilience is an active process that is continually evolving, and never perfectly achieved. Tomorrow is another day to try anew. It is like working in my yard during the summer time. My goal is to create a beautiful space that the whole family can enjoy, but I never have enough time to finish the mowing, weeding, trimming, watering, and planting. I have to accept the fact that whatever I *can* get done any given day needs to be "good enough." You have your goals, too, and they are important to aim for. At the end of the day, however, so long as you are following your values and doing your best, whatever you are doing with your loved one needs to be good enough. The Wilsons told this story:

> We were informal caregivers for our neighbors, Sol and Maddie. Sol was physically frail and his wife had some kind of memory problems. Their large extended family was devoted, but trying to juggle their own busy lives. In the beginning, we would do occasional friendly things, like having meals together on holidays or special occasions. Little by little, though, there was more to take on. We would mow the lawn and dig up the dandelions from their yard, taking care to close the gate so Maddie wouldn't wander away. We got in the habit of taking out and bringing in the garbage cans every week. Eventually, we were picking up and delivering

their mail, stopping to chat whenever we had time after dropping it off. Our kids would come and play with the couple's two dogs; our eldest boy would watch sports events with Sol on the big-screen TV at his house. When we'd visit, we'd give the dishes an extra good cleaning and the counters a swipe. We occasionally picked up their groceries and shoveled their driveway on snow days. It never seemed enough, though. Sol was lonely and we always felt guilty that we didn't spend more time with him. After Sol and Maddie finally had to move into a nursing home, we got a call from their family, thanking us for our help over the years. They didn't remember all the things we hadn't done for the old couple. They were just grateful that we had cared enough about Sol and Maddie to be there when we could.

The third and final secret is to always remember that you are not alone. Reach out to other people. Let those family and friends who love you show that love by helping as they can. Ask for assistance from community agencies and programs that are there to serve you. Millions of men and women around the world are facing the challenge of living with dementia, and we all need to lean on one another for support and encouragement to figure out the best way to care for the people we love. It is true that establishing new habits, including the skill of asking for and accepting help from others, takes practice. However, all of the strategies I have talked about in this book become easier over time. I once heard a motivational speaker talk about how difficult it is to get into the habit of flossing one's teeth. If changing something so small as starting to floss one's teeth is so challenging, no wonder it can seem impossible to stay resilient in the midst of the ever-changing world of dementia care. But you *can* do it. Resilience does not mean perfection or always knowing what to do. If you can trust your values and reach out to those around you, you will be better poised to keep your perspective and handle whatever challenges come your way.

In this book, I have tried to give you an easy-to-remember set of tools that will help you keep your perspective as you care for your loved one with dementia. No two situations are the same. However, caregivers who learn to D.A.N.C.E. with the person they are caring for will become more resilient—able to recover from or adjust to change, and be more buoyant in the face of difficulties and challenges. There is no one right way to provide quality dementia care. Resilience is being able to dance with your loved one, no matter where he or she is leading. When you do that, you, like Dr. Carl in the story below, may find yourself in an unexpectedly beautiful place that you would have never been able to find alone.

Dr. Carl was professor emeritus at a major university. For years, he had been working on a book in his area of expertise. His wife's declining health and memory had taken up much of his time, however, and it was only after she was admitted to a nursing home that he was able to return to it. One day, when Dr. Carl went to visit his wife, she unexpectedly asked, "Did you ever finish that book?" Dr. Carl was very surprised that his wife remembered that he had been writing a book. When they had been a young academic couple, his wife often helped edit his papers and manuscripts, putting little notes and comments in the margins, but it had been many years since she seemed fully cognizant of what was going on around her. Nevertheless, he replied, "Yes, as a matter of fact, my book has just been published." To Dr. Carl's further amazement, his wife said, "I want a copy." So he brought her one. Over the months ahead, the nurses reported to Dr. Carl that his wife often sat in her chair with the book open in her lap. No one believed she could actually read it, and half the time she was just sitting asleep holding it, but it seemed to be important to her to have the book nearby. Eventually, Dr. Carl's wife died. When he went to the nursing home to pick up his wife's belongings, he found the book. He distractedly opened it up to the acknowledgments page, where he had dedicated the book to his wife with love. There in the margin, in his wife's shaky handwriting, were the words, "Good job."

Appendix: Caregiver Resources

GENERAL INFORMATION ABOUT ALZHEIMER'S DISEASE

Alzheimer's Association

Telephone Number: 1-800-272-3900

Web site: http://www.alz.org

Offers information about support groups, educational programs and materials, case management, and community resources for AD patients and caregivers.

Alzheimer's Disease Education and Referral Center (ADEAR)

Telephone Number: 1-800-438-4380

Web site: http://www.alzheimers.org

Provides educational materials and information produced by the National Institute on Aging and Alzheimer's Disease Research Centers.

Area Agencies on Aging (AAA)

Telephone Number: 1-800-677-1116 (9:00 AM-8:00 PM, EST) for Senior Information and Assistance; check your local government listings for other AAA services.

Web site: http://www.aoa.dhhs.gov

Offices in every state provide information and assistance regarding local resources for older adults, including Aging and Adult Services, Senior Information and Assistance, and Adult Protective Services. These agencies can also assist in applying for Medicaid.

American Association for Retired Persons (AARP)

Telephone Number: 1-888-687-2277

Web site: http://www.aarp.org

Provides general information on topics pertinent to persons over age fifty-five, with a link to family caregiving topics.

American Health Assistance Foundation (AHAF)

Telephone Number: 1-800-437-2423

Web site: http://www.ahaf.org

Provides information about Alzheimer's disease family relief programs.

Mayo Clinic Health Page

Web site: http://www.mayoclinic.com

Nationally recognized web page with links to health topics, including Alzheimer's disease and an "ask the expert" page.

National Alliance for Caregiving (NAC)

Web site: www.caregiving.org

National Family Caregivers Association (NFCA)

Telephone Number: 1-800-896-3650

Web site: http://www.edc.gsph.pitt.edu/reach

Operated in conjunction with the NIH REACH (Resources for Enhancing Alzheimer's Caregiver Health) program.

NIH Senior Health

Web site: http://www.nihseniorhealth.gov

Provides information through the National Institutes on Health on a wide range of health-related topics, with links to Alzheimer's disease and caregiving.

Positive Aging Resource Center (PARC)

Web site: http://positiveaging.org

Provides evidence-based information for both caregivers and health care professionals about healthy aging.

COMMON COMMUNITY SUPPORT SERVICES

Adult Day Care or Day Health Care

Consult local Alzheimer's Association or Area Agency on Aging for programs suitable for dementia patients.

Provides daytime social activities, therapy, health care, and supervision in a group setting, often in a community center, church, or nursing home. Transportation is sometimes available; hours and fees vary.

Case Management

Telephone Number: See business section of local directory under "Case Management." Local Alzheimer's Association or AAA may also provide services.

National Association of Professional Geriatric Care managers:

Telephone Number: 1-520-881-8008

Web site: http://www.caremanager.org

Case managers may be nurses, social workers, or other professionals trained in assessing an individual's needs and making appropriate recommendations. This is an especially good resource for families that do not live in the same town as the patient, or for caregivers who are overwhelmed.

Home Chore Services

Telephone Number: Check yellow pages, or consult local Area Agency on Aging case manager.

These agencies provide chore, personal care, and companion services for individuals living at home.

Home Health-Care Agencies

Telephone Number: Check yellow pages, under "Home Health."

These agencies provide in-home monitoring, treatment, therapies, etc., authorized by a physician. Services are usually provided by nurses, physical therapists, or trained aides.

Legal Services

Your state bar association can provide information about attorneys who specialize in elder law. The local Alzheimer's Association may also have information about low-cost legal assistance.

Families often need to consult with an attorney trained in elder law regarding powers of attorney, guardianship, and other legal and financial issues.

Overnight Respite

Local Area Agency on Aging or Alzheimer's Association can provide information about respite in your community.

Overnight care for individuals with dementia may be provided by local skilled nursing facilities (nursing homes), assisted-living facilities, or adult family homes.

© Modified from Logsdon et al., 1997; reprinted with permission.

Notes

Chapter 1. Why Resilience Matters

1. *The Random House Dictionary of the English Language* (1966). Several authors have used the "coiled wire" metaphor to discuss the concept of resilience as it relates to the challenges of living with aging, illness, and loss (Felten & Hall, 2001; Jacelon, 1997).

2. For an alternative but related descriptive categorization of caregiver types based upon caregiver management strategies, see de Vugt et al. (2004) and their discussion of nonadapters, nurturers, and supporters.

3. A recent survey of 603 older adults (Hardy, Concato, & Gill, 2002) who had experienced similar, stressful life events during the past five years found that there was wide variability in the older persons' perception of whether these stresses had produced positive or negative consequences for their lives. Negative evaluations were associated with higher levels of depression and loss of functional independence. There is a growing literature showing that mood, health, and ability to cope with the challenges of dementia care are similarly highly correlated with caregivers' appraisal of their situation (Dilworth-Anderson & Gibson, 2002; Hooker et al., 2002; Lee, Brennan, & Daly, 2001; Mahoney, Tarlow, & Jones, 2003; Martin-Cook, Remakel-Davis, Svetlik, Hynan, & Weiner, 2003; Mittelman, Roth, Haley, & Zarit, 2004; Nolan, Ingram, & Watson, 2003).

4. Variability in caregivers' appraisal of a stressful situation is caused, in part, by differences in their ability to "step back" and see their situation in the context of the larger world reality. This is reminiscent of the term "cognitive empathy" (Lee et al., 2001), which is the ability to understand another person's feelings and experiences while maintaining an objective distance or sense of perspective. For caregivers, the challenge is to keep that perspective with regard to their *own* thoughts, feelings, and experiences. Hayes, Strosahl, and Wilson (1999) use metaphors to help clients grasp the subtle distinction. For example, thinking a negative phrase such as "This situation is hopeless" or "I can't take it anymore" is a very different experience from viewing those same phrases typed on a computer screen

in front of you. In the latter case, a person is "looking at" their thoughts or feelings, as opposed to "looking through" the literal meaning of these experiences. This psychological shift makes it much more likely that the person will discover alternative ways to respond to their situation. With practice, this ability to step back, to "see the forest not just the trees," can become more habitual.

5. For a more comprehensive discussion of the evolution of the resilience construct, see reviews by Jacelon (1997) and Tusaie and Dyer (2004).

6. Personality characteristics associated with stress-resilience in older adults can be found in many works (Connor & Davidson, 2003; Hardy, Concato, & Gill, 2004; Roberts & Cleveland, 2001; Wagnild, 2003; Wagnild & Young, 1993). Wagnild and Young (1990) coined the phrase "emotional stamina" to describe resilience. Charney (2004) has written eloquently about the potential relationship between resilience and neurobiological function.

7. In its brochure on resilience, the American Psychological Association (2003) points out that people commonly demonstrate resilience in stressful situations. Questions in the APA brochure designed to help readers reflect on their past experiences and successes as a way of understanding and responding to current crises provide an outline for the resilience exercise included at the end of this chapter.

8. The approach taken throughout this book, that resilience is a dynamic, multidimensional skill that can be learned by anyone at any stage of life, has growing clinical and scientific support (American Psychological Association, 2003; Connor & Davidson, 2003; Flach, 1989; Rutter, 1985), although the body of research is less developed than that for trait theories of resilience. Readers interested in exploring the historical basis for the process of resilience might consider the work of early theorists who viewed adult development as an interaction between one's personality and environmental stressors or major life events (cf. Bowers, 1973; Riegel, 1975).

9. The *American Journal of Cardiology* published an article about an eighty-one-year-old man who had competed in 591 marathons (Brendle, Joseph, Sorkin, McNelly, & Katzel, 2003). Perhaps most amazing of all, he ran his first marathon at age forty-nine. This story is a fabulous example of how human beings at any age are capable of accomplishing almost anything, given purpose and determination.

10. Examples of how the construct of resilience can be used in phenomenological or clinical studies of aging and caregiving can be found in Roberts and Cleveland (2001) and Shapiro (2002).

11. The Duke studies used a relatively new instrument, the Connor-Davidson Resilience Scale (CD-RISC), to measure resilience in their subjects. See Connor and Davidson (2003) for details on the psychometric development of the

CD-RISC, and subsequent articles on its use in clinical trials and community surveys (Connor, Davidson, & Lee, 2003; Davidson et al., 2005).

12. The Resilience Scale was first published in Wagnild and Young (1993). Translations into Spanish and Russian have been described (Aroian, Schappler-Morris, Neary, Spitzer, & Tran, 1997; Heilemann, Lee, & Kury, 2003). Although the Resilience Scale has particular applicability to older adults, and has been used descriptively in studies with dementia caregivers (Garity, 1997), there are no data to date on its use in clinical outcome trials.

13. Cowen (2001) has pointed out that studying resilience is challenging because there is no universal operational definition for what constitutes good adjustment (or adaptation or competence) in a given individual, and no simple way to handle the fact that people often have very different perceptions on the stressfulness of a given situation. The availability of standardized measures of resilience (e.g., those by Connor & Davidson, 2003; Friborg, Hjemdal, Rosenvinge, & Martinussen, 2003; Hardy et al., 2004; Wagnild & Young, 1993) is a start on addressing this problem, although they have not been widely used to date. I think Tusaie and Dyer (2004) correctly note that resilience may be best measured by a combination of quantitative assessments using scales such as the CD-RISC or Resilience Scale, that are correlated to outcomes relevant to a given population (e.g., caregivers), and combined with qualitative assessments that can examine the unique dynamics of resilience across individuals.

14. Erikson (1959).

Chapter 2. D: Don't Argue!

1. For a scholarly discussion of the complex issues of communication changes in normal aging and dementia, see Bayles and Kaszniak (1987).

2. Oliver Sacks describes a particularly striking example of agnosia in *The Man Who Mistook His Wife for a Hat* (1998).

3. The Serenity Prayer most widely associated with Alcoholics Anonymous is, "God help me to change the things I have the power to change, to accept the things I cannot change, and the wisdom to know the difference." The pertinence of acceptance in dementia caregiving is discussed in detail in Chapter 3 of this book.

4. I first heard the quotation, "Don't just do something, stand there," from Dea Eisner, MD, Tacoma, WA.

5. This conceptualization of interpersonal tolerance was given to me by Chris McCurry, PhD.

6. A recent study described the ten most common communication strategies recommended in the literature for helping persons with dementia, and also looked

at the relative frequency with which caregivers actually use these strategies (Small & Gutman, 2002).

7. This quotation is taken from a training program developed by Dr. Teri and her colleagues for staff in assisted-living residences (Teri & Piruz, 2002).

8. The clinician friend referred to here is Steve Graybar, PhD, Reno, Nevada.

9. I heard a story similar to this one told years ago by Wendy Lustbader, MSW, at an Alzheimer's Association education conference. Readers interested in reading more about Wendy's highly compassionate and thoughtful approach to aging and dementia care are encouraged to read some of her books, such as *Counting on Kindness* (1993) and *What's Worth Knowing* (2004).

Chapter 3. A: Accept the Disease

1. McCormick et al. (1995).

2. The American Academy of Neurology (Knopman et al., 2001) has issued practice standards for the diagnosis of dementia that include screening for depression, B_{12} deficiency, and hypothyroidism. Structural neuroimaging with either a noncontrast Computed Tomography (CT) scan or Magnetic Resonance Imaging (MRI) to look for evidence of strokes or other structural brain diseases that might be causing the clinical symptoms is also recommended. The deleterious effect of medications on cognition in older adults has been widely described (cf. Brown & Stoudemire, 1998; Tune, 2001).

3. See the paper by Rosen et al. (2002) on the rates of primary providers who are not practicing recommended guidelines for dementia diagnosis and follow-up. The survey suggests that the Joneses' experience of having their concerns not taken seriously by their provider is uncommon, although it does happen. More common is providers' failure to provide education about, and assistance with, follow-up services. Fahy, Wald, Walker, and Livingston (2003) address the issue of physicians who withhold the dementia diagnosis because of *caregiver* preferences, rather than their own discomfort with the feedback process.

4. Multiple professional medical groups, including the American Academy of Neurology, the American Psychiatric Association, and the Canadian Medical Association, have issued practice guidelines to assist primary providers in the diagnosis and management of dementing illnesses (cf. Doody et al., 2001; Knopman et al., 2001; Patterson et al., 1999).

5. Portions of this section are modified from a Realistic Expectations handout that has been used in the University of Washington research protocols treating mood and behavior disturbances in Alzheimer's disease (cf. Teri, McCurry, Logsdon, Huda, & Korkowski, 2003).

6. For discussion of some of the risk factors and rates of elder mistreatment among caregivers of persons with dementia, see Anetzberger et al. (2000), Fulmer (2002), Beach, Schulz, Williamson, Miller, Weiner, & Lance (2005), and Williamson and Shaffer (2001).

7. I published a case study several years ago describing a situation in which a caregiver died because his demented wife failed to summon appropriate aid when he suffered a medical crisis (McCurry & Teri, 1997). Caregivers often plan ahead for how best to care for their loved one at various stages of dementia, but neglect to consider the serious problem of whether their loved one is capable of responding to an emergency if the caregiver is incapacitated.

8. The specific use of a twelve-step philosophy for dementia caregivers has been written about in greater detail elsewhere. Interested readers are referred to Farran and Keane-Hagerty (1989) and Samples, D. Larsen, and M. Larsen (2000). "Accepting one day at a time" is from the Serenity Prayer commonly associated with Alcoholics Anonymous, and was first used in a prayer written by the theologian Reinhold Niebuhr (1892–1971).

9. For a review of the relationship between emotional willingness or acceptance and positive outcomes in therapy, see Hayes, Wilson, Gifford, Follette, and Strosahl (1996). Examples of modern acceptance-based therapeutic approaches include Acceptance and Commitment Therapy (ACT) (Hayes, Strosahl, and Wilson, 1999), Dialectical Behavior Therapy (DBT) (Koerner & Linehan, 2000), Functional Analytic psychotherapy (Kohlenberg & Tsai, 1991), and Integrative Behavioral Couple Therapy (Jacobson, Christensen, Prince, Cordova, & Eldridge, 2000). These as well as other acceptance-oriented theorists and clinicians were part of the 1993 Nevada Conference on Acceptance and Change, Reno, NV, for which proceedings have been published (Hayes, Jacobson, Follette, & Dougher, 1994).

10. I am most familiar with the Acceptance and Commitment Therapy (ACT) approach, which was developed by my major advisor in graduate school (Steven C. Hayes, PhD). Over the past decade, Dr. Hayes and his colleagues have trained hundreds of clinicians around the world in the underlying philosophy and application of ACT with a wide variety of clinical populations. Readers interested in finding out more specifics about ACT, including its underlying philosophy of science, and foundation in behavior analysis, are encouraged to read Hayes, Strosahl, and Wilson (1999). A review of the empirical studies to date using ACT as a therapeutic modality has been recently published (Hayes, Masuda, Bissett, Luoma, & Guerrero, 2004).

Chapter 4. N: Nurture Yourself

1. *The 36-Hour Day* (Mace & Rabins, 1981), a classic, now in its third edition, has been translated and published all over the world.

2. For reviews of the medical and psychological comorbidity associated with dementia caregiving, see Pinquart and Sorensen (2003a, 2003b), Schulz and Martire (2004), and Vitaliano, Zhang, and Scanlan (2003).

3. One of the earliest investigators to coin the term "hidden patients" for caregivers was Haug (1994).

4. Numerous studies have looked at the use of relaxation or meditation in alleviating the stress of family caregivers (Fisher & Laschinger, 2001; Mizuno, Hosak, Ogihara, Higano, & Mano, 1999; Waelde, Thompson, & Gallagher-Thompson, 2004). I myself have used it as part of a package to improve nighttime sleep in caregivers (McCurry, Logsdon, Vitiello, & Teri, 1998).

5. Tips for Learning to Relax is modified from a treatment manual that we have used at the University of Washington (Logsdon, McCurry, & Teri, 2003).

6. The QOL-AD, including reliability and validity data can be found in Logsdon, Gibbons, McCurry, and Teri (1999).

7. A series of papers describe the relationship between depression, residential situation, quality of life, and lack of pleasant events (Logsdon & Albert, 1999; Logsdon, Gibbons, McCurry, & Teri, 2002, 2004; and Logsdon, Gibbons, & Teri, 2001; Teri, McCurry, Logsdon, & Gibbons, in press).

8. I first heard this insight years ago in a talk given by Joanne Rader, who has written eloquently on the importance of individualized dementia care for persons with dementia living in long-term care settings (Rader & Tornquist, 1995).

9. This quote by Wendy Lustbader is found on p. 201 in a book by Goldman (2002) that contains a number of moving stories by family caregivers.

10. The paper, "What I want if I get Alzheimer's disease" (Reifler, 1995), was written in the form of a letter to Dr. Reifler's wife. Persons interested in obtaining respite services should contact their local Area Agency on Aging (AAA) for locations, costs, eligibility requirements, and listings of available services. *Consumer Reports* has also published a very useful overview of the issues involved (Lieberman & Editors at Consumer Reports Bureau, 2000).

Chapter 5. C: Create Novel Solutions

1. Linda Pinsky, MD, a physician-educator at the University of Washington, and one of the more creative people I know, has greatly shaped my thinking about the process of creative problem solving.

2. *The Blind Man and the Elephant* by John Godfrey Saxe is based upon a fable from the Udana, a canonical Hindu scripture.

3. Numerous authors have written about how creative thinking has evolved and can be taught (Price, 2004; Wasserman, Young, & Cook, 2004).

4. Neuringer (2004) has postulated that creativity, that is, diversity in responding, is a learned behavior that is shaped by the same reinforcement principles underlying other kinds of more stereotyped learned behaviors.

5. The observation that caregivers are not necessarily good reporters of their loved one's sleeping patterns (McCurry, Vitiello, Gibbons, Logsdon, & Teri, in press) is reminiscent of a larger research on caregiver appraisal, which examines how caregivers' perspective on their situation affects their ability to cope with dementia-related behavior problems and benefit from psychoeducational treatments.

6. Teri and Logsdon (2000); Teri, Logsdon, and McCurry (2002).

7. For reviews of the literature on psychosocial treatments for dementia, see Bartels et al. (2002) and Cohen-Mansfield (2001). At University of Washington, we have developed a series of interventions based upon a core group of behavioral principles, applied to specific problem areas (the "Seattle Protocols"; Teri, Logsdon, & McCurry, 2005), including depression (Teri, Logsdon, Uomoto, & McCurry, 1997), agitation (Teri et al., 1998), physical inactivity (Teri, Gibbons, et al., 2003), and sleep (McCurry, Gibbons, Logsdon, Vitiello, & Teri, 2005).

Chapter 6. E: Enjoy the Moment

1. See Albert et al. (1996) for more information on Dr. Albert's work on quality of life in late-stage dementia.

2. Teri et al., 1997.

3. Studies that have looked at individualized pleasant activities and quality of life in nursing homes include Bell et al. (2004); Reimer, Slaughter, Donaldson, Currie, and Eliaziw (2004); Richards, Sullivan, Phillips, Beck, and Overton-McCoy (2001). For studies examining the use of complementary therapies, see Grasel, Wiltfang, and Kornhuber (2003); Snow, Hovanec, and Brandt (2004); Thorgrimsen, Spector, Wiles, and Orrell (2003); and Vink, Birks, Bruinsma, and Scholten (2004).

4. A description of the PES-AD, including its original longer version and information on its psychometric properties, can be found in Teri and Logsdon (1991), and Logsdon and Teri (1997).

5. Taken from a training program developed by Dr. Teri and her colleagues for staff in assisted-living residences (Teri & Piruz, 2002).

6. A number of gerontological researchers have written about the uplifts in caregiving and their relationship to mental/physical functioning of caregivers (Gold et al., 1995; Kinney & Stephens, 1989; Lawrence, Tennstedt, & Assmann, 1998; Lawton, Moss, Kleban, Glicksman, & Rovine, 1991; Pinquart & Sorensen, 2003a, 2004).

7. Nolan, Ryan, Enderby, and Reid (2002).

8. Gallagher-Thompson, Dal Canto, Jacob, and Thompson (2001).

9. Frankl's classic work *Man's Search for Meaning* (1984) describes the genesis and development of an approach to psychiatric therapy, which he calls "logotherapy." Drawing upon his experiences as a prisoner of war in the Nazi death camps, Dr. Frankl maintains that humans can transcend suffering and find meaning in life, regardless of the circumstances. From this perspective, there are three main ways a person can find meaning: creating a work or doing a deed; encountering another human being in love; and facing a fate that you cannot change, and rising above it, growing beyond suffering to turn personal tragedy into triumph. The pertinence of logotherapy to many aspects of aging—facing retirement, bereavement, or caregiving—is apparent. Dr. Farran has used Frankl's constructs to develop the Finding Meaning Through Caregiving Scale (FMTCS). For more detailed information on the FMTCS, see Farran, Keane-Hagerty, Salloway, Kupferer, and Wilken (1991); and Farran, Miller, Kaufman, Donner, and Fogg (1999).

10. These common caregiver themes were reported as part of a phenomenological study at Rush University (Paun, 2004) that explored the role of spirituality in African-American and Caucasian caregivers.

11. For example, gratitude is the core of Naikan therapy (cf. Reynolds, 1989), a meditative practice in which persons are guided to reflect on key persons in one's life, considering not only the problems they have caused you, but also the services these persons did for you and the trouble you caused them in return. Thus, Naikan emphasizes a balanced recognition of the ways in which people have helped and continue to help us in concrete ways that we frequently fail to acknowledge or appreciate. Gratitude, where it is due, leads naturally to a desire to help others, helping the sufferer to focus attention away from self to the larger world around him or her.

12. *Solitude* (Wilcox, 1919).

13. In addition to Norman Cousins' classic (1979), see review on humor in medicine by Bennett (2003), and books by other authors describing the place for humor and joy in caring for persons with Alzheimer's disease (Brackey, 2004; Murphy & Clark, 1998).

14. The original version of the PES-AD published in 1991 contained 53 items; the version presented in this book was developed and copyrighted in 1996.

Section III. The Promise: You Can Do It!

1. Cf. *The Silver Palate Cookbook* (Rosso, Lukins, & McLaughlin, 1979, p. 129).

2. Prochaska's and DiClemente's Transtheoretical Model of Behavior Change (Prochaska, DiClemente, & Norcross, 1992) was developed to help understand how and why people change. The model, which is widely used in behavioral medicine, divides the readiness to change into six stages, which people often cycle through many times before a change becomes habit.

Bibliography

Albert, S. M., Del Castillo-Castaneda, C., Sano, M., Jacobs, D. M., Marder, K., Bell, K., et al. (1996). Quality of life in patients with Alzheimer's disease as reported by patient proxies. *Journal of the American Geriatrics Society, 44*(11), 1342–1347.

American Psychiatric Association. (1997). Practice guidelines for the treatment of patients with Alzheimer's disease and other dementias of late life. *American Journal of Psychiatry, 154*(Suppl. 5), 1–39.

American Psychological Association. (2003). *The road to resilience.* Washington, DC: Author.

Anetzberger, G. J., Palmisano, B. R., Sanders, M., Bass, D., Dayton, C., Eckert, S., et al. (2000). A model intervention for elder abuse and dementia. *The Gerontologist, 40*(4), 492–497.

Aroian, K. J., Schappler-Morris, N., Neary, S., Spitzer, A., & Tran, T. V. (1997). Psychometric evaluation of the Russian language version of the Resilience Scale. *Journal of Nursing Measurement, 5*(2), 151–164.

Avadian, B. (2002). *Finding the JOY in Alzheimer's: Vol. 1. Caregivers share the joyful times.* Lancaster, CA: North Star Books.

Avadian, B. (2003). *Finding the JOY in Alzheimer's: Vol. 2. When tears are dried with laughter.* Lancaster, CA: North Star Books.

Bartels, S. J., Dums, A. R., Oxman, T. E., Schneider, L. S., Arean, P. A., Alexopoulos, G. S., et al. (2002). Evidence-based practices in geriatric mental health care. *Psychiatric Services, 53*(11), 1419–1431.

Bayles, K. A., & Kaszniak, A. W. (1987). *Communication and cognition in normal aging and dementia.* Austin, TX: PRO-ED.

Beach, S. R., Schulz, R., Williamson, G. M., Miller, L. S., Weiner, M. F., & Lance, C. E. (2005). Risk factors for potentially harmful informal caregiver behavior. *Journal of the American Geriatrics Society, 53*(2), 255–261.

Bell, V., Troxel, D., Hamon, R., & Cox, T. (2004). *The best friends book of Alzheimer's activities!* Towson, MD: Health Professions Press.

Bennett, H. J. (2003). Humor in medicine. *Southern Medical Journal, 96*(12), 1257–1261.

Bowers, K. S. (1973). Situationalism in psychology. *Psychological Review, 80*(3), 307–336.

Brackey, J. (2004). *Creating moments of joy: A journal for caregivers.* West Lafayette, IN: Purdue University Press.

Brendle, D. C., Joseph, L.J.O., Sorkin, J. D., McNelly, D., & Katzel, L. I. (2003). Aging and marathon times in an 81-year-old man who competed in 591 marathons. *American Journal of Cardiology, 91*(9), 1154–1156.

Brown, T. M., & Stoudemire, A. (1998). *Psychiatric side effects of prescription and over-the-counter medications: Recognition and management.* Arlington, VA: American Psychiatric Publishing.

Charney, D. S. (2004). Psychobiological mechanisms of resilience and vulnerability: Implications for successful adaptation to extreme stress. *American Journal of Psychiatry, 161*(2), 195–216.

Cohen-Mansfield, J. (2001). Nonpharmacologic interventions for inappropriate behaviors in dementia. *American Journal of Geriatric Psychiatry, 9*(4), 361–381.

Connor, K. M., & Davidson, J.R.T. (2003). Development of a new resilience scale: The Connor-Davidson Resilience Scale (CD-RISC). *Depression and Anxiety, 18*(2), 76–82.

Connor, K. M., Davidson, J.R.T., & Lee, L. C. (2003). Spirituality, resilience, and anger in survivors of violent trauma: A community survey. *Journal of Traumatic Stress, 16*(5), 487–494.

Cousins, N. (1979). *Anatomy of an illness as perceived by the patient: Reflections on healing and regeneration.* New York: W. W. Norton.

Cowen, E. L. (2001). Ethics in community mental health care. *Community Mental Health Journal, 37*(1), 3–13.

Davidson, J. R., Payne, V. M., Connor, K. M., Foa, E. B., Rothbaum, B. O., Hertzberg, M. A., et al. (2005). Trauma, resilience and saliostasis: Effects of treatment in post-traumatic stress disorder. *International Clinical Psychopharmacology, 20*(1), 43–48.

de Vugt, M., Stevens, F., Aalten, P., Lousberg, R., Jaspers, N., Winkens, I., et al. (2004). Do caregiver management strategies influence patient behavior in dementia? *International Journal of Geriatric Psychiatry, 19*(1), 85–92.

Dilworth-Anderson, P., & Gibson, B. E. (2002). The cultural influence of values, norms, meanings, and perceptions in understanding dementia in ethnic minorities. *Alzheimer Disease and Associated Disorders, 16*(Suppl. 2), S56–S63.

Doody, R. S., Stevens, J. C., Beck, C., Dubinsky, R. M., Kaye, J. A., Gwyther, L., et al. (2001). Practice parameter: Management of dementia (an evidence-based review). Report of the Quality Standards Subcommittee of the American Academy of Neurology. *Neurology, 56*(9), 1154–1166.

Erikson, E. H. (1959). Identity and the life cycle. *Psychological Issues, 1*(1), 50–100.

Fahy, M., Wald, C., Walker, Z., & Livingston, G. (2003). Secrets and lies: The dilemma of disclosing the diagnosis to an adult with dementia. *Age and Ageing, 32*(4), 439–441.

Farran, C. J., & Keane-Hagerty, E. (1989). Twelve steps for caregivers. *The American Journal of Alzheimer's Care and Related Disorders & Research,* (November/December), 38–41.

Farran, C. J., Keane-Hagerty, E., Salloway, S., Kupferer, S., & Wilken, C. S. (1991). Finding meaning: An alternative paradigm for Alzheimer's disease family caregivers. *The Gerontologist, 31*(4), 483–489.

Farran, C. J., Miller, B. H., Kaufman, J. E., Donner, E., & Fogg, L. (1999). Finding meaning through caregiving: Development of an instrument for family caregivers of persons with Alzheimer's disease. *Journal of Clinical Psychology, 55*(9), 1107–1125.

Felten, B. S., & Hall, J. M. (2001). Conceptualizing resilience in women older than 85. *Journal of Gerontological Nursing, 27*(11), 46–53.

Fisher, P. A., & Laschinger, H. S. (2001). A relaxation training program to increase self-efficacy for anxiety control in Alzheimer family caregivers. *Holistic Nursing Practice, 15*(2), 47–58.

Flach, F. F. (1989). *Resilience: Discovering a new strength at times of stress.* New York: Fawcett Columbine.

Frankl, V. (1984). *Man's search for meaning.* New York: Simon & Schuster.

Friborg, O., Hjemdal, O., Rosenvinge, J. H., & Martinussen, M. (2003). A new rating scale for adult resilience: What are the central protective resources behind healthy adjustment? *International Journal of Methods in Psychiatric Research, 12*(2), 65–76.

Fulmer, T. (2002). Elder mistreatment. *Annual Review of Nursing Research, 20,* 369–395.

Gallagher-Thompson, D., Dal Canto, P. G., Jacob, T., & Thompson, L. W. (2001). A comparison of marital interaction patterns between couples in which the husband does or does not have Alzheimer's disease. *Journal of Gerontology: Social Sciences, 56*(3), S140–S150.

Garity, J. (1997). Stress, learning syle, resilience factors, and ways of coping in Alzheimer family caregivers. *American Journal of Alzheimer's Disease, 12*(4), 171–178.

Gold, D. P., Cohen, C., Shulman, K., Zucchero, C., Andres, D., & Etezadi, J. (1995). Caregiving and dementia: Predicting negative and positive outcomes for caregivers. *International Journal of Aging and Human Development, 41*(3), 183–201.

Goldman, C. (2002). *The gifts of caregiving.* Minneapolis, MN: Fairview Press.

Grasel, E., Wiltfang, J., & Kornhuber, J. (2003). Non-drug therapies for dementia: An overview of the current situation with regard to proof of effectiveness. *Dementia and Geriatric Cognitive Disorders, 15*(3), 115–125.

Hardy, S. E., Concato, J., & Gill, T. M. (2004). Resilience of community-dwelling older persons. *Journal of the American Geriatrics Society, 52*(2), 257–262.

Hardy, S. E., Concato, J., & Gill, T. M. (2002). Stressful life events among community-living older persons. *Journal of General Internal Medicine, 17*(11), 832–838.

Haug, M. R. (1994). Elderly patients, caregivers, and physicians: Theory and research on health care triads. *Journal of Health and Social Behavior, 35*(1), 1–12.

Hayes, S. C., Jacobson, N. S., Follette, V. M., & Dougher, M. J. (Eds.). (1994). *Acceptance and change: Content and context in psychotherapy.* Reno, NV: Context Press.

Hayes, S. C., Masuda, A., Bissett, R., Luoma, J., & Guerrero, L. F. (2004). DBT, FAR, and ACT: How empirically oriented are the new behavior therapy technologies? *Behavior Therapy, 35*(1), 35–54.

Hayes, S. C., Strosahl, K. D., & Wilson, K. G. (1999). *Acceptance and commitment therapy: An experiential approach to behavior change.* New York: Guilford Press.

Hayes, S. C., Wilson, K. G., Gifford, E. V., Follette, V. M., & Strosahl, K. (1996). Experiential avoidance and behavioral disorders: A functional dimensional approach to diagnosis and treatment. *Journal of Consulting and Clinical Psychology, 64*(6), 1152–1168.

Heilemann, M. V., Lee, K., & Kury, F. S. (2003). Psychometric properties of the Spanish version of the Resilience Scale. *Journal of Nursing Measurement, 11*(1), 61–72.

Hooker, K., Bowman, S. R., Coehlo, D. P., Lim, S. R., Jeffrey, K., Guariglia, R., et al. (2002). Behavioral change in persons with dementia: Relationships with mental and physical health of caregivers. *Journal of Gerontology: Psychological Sciences, 57B*(5), P454–P460.

Jacelon, C. S. (1997). The trait and process of resilience. *Journal of Advanced Nursing, 25*(1), 123–129.

Jacobson, N. S., Christensen, A., Prince, S. E., Cordova, J., & Eldridge, K. (2000). Integrative behavioral couple therapy: An acceptance-based, promising new treatment for couple discord. *Journal of Consulting and Clinical Psychology, 68*(2), 351–355.

Kinney, J. M., & Stephens, M.A.P. (1989). Hassles and uplifts of giving care to a family member with dementia. *Psychology and Aging, 4*(4), 402–408.

Knopman, D. S., DeKosky, S. T., Cummings, J. L., Chui, H., Corey-Bloom, J., Relkin, N., et al. (2001). *Practice parameter: Diagnosis of dementia (an evidence-based review).* Report of the Quality Standards Subcommittee of the American Academy of Neurology. *Neurology, 56*(9), 1143–1153.

Koerner, K., & Linehan, M. M. (2000). Research on dialectical behavior therapy for patients with borderline personality disorder. *Psychiatric Clinics of North America, 23*(1): 151–167.

Kohlenberg, R. J., & Tsai, M. (1991). *Functional analytic psychotherapy: Creating intense and curative therapeutic relationships.* Cambridge, MA: Perseus Publishing.

Lawrence, R. H., Tennstedt, S. L., & Assmann, S. F. (1998). Quality of the caregiver–care recipient relationship: Does it offset negative consequences of caregiving for family caregivers? *Psychology and Aging, 13*(1), 150–158.

Lawton, M. P., Moss, M., Kleban, M. H., Glicksman, A., & Rovine, M. (1991). A two-factor model of caregiving appraisal and psychological well-being. *Journal of Gerontology: Psychological Sciences, 46*(4), P181–P189.

Lee, H. S., Brennan, P. F., & Daly, B. J. (2001). Relationship of empathy to appraisal, depression, life satisfaction, and physical health in informal caregivers of older adults. *Research in Nursing and Health, 24*(1), 44–56.

Lieberman, T., & Editors at Consumer Reports Bureau. (2000). *Consumer reports complete guide to heatlh services for seniors.* New York: Crown Publishing Group.

Logsdon, R. G., & Albert, S. M. (1999). Assessing quality of life in Alzheimer's disease: Conceptual and methodological issues. *Journal of Mental Health and Aging, 5*(1), 3–6.

Logsdon, R. G., Gibbons, L. E., McCurry, S. M., & Teri, L. (July 2004). *Assessing changes in quality of life in Alzheimer's disease.* Paper presented at the Ninth International Conference on Alzheimer's Disease and Related Disorders, Philadelphia, PA.

Logsdon, R. G., Gibbons, L. E., McCurry, S. M., & Teri, L. (2002). Assessing quality of life in older adults with cognitive impairment. *Psychosomatic Medicine, 64*, 510–519.

Logsdon, R. G., Gibbons, L. E., McCurry, S. M., & Teri, L. (1999). Quality of life in Alzheimer's disease: Patient and caregiver reports. *Journal of Mental Health and Aging, 5*(1), 21–32.

Logsdon, R. G., Gibbons, L. E., & Teri, L. (August 2001). *Enhancing quality of life in assisted living facilities.* Paper presented at the American Psychological Association meeting, San Francisco, CA.

Logsdon, R. G., McCurry, S. M., & Teri, L. (2003). *RALLI: Resources and activities for life long independence.* Seattle: University of Washington.

Logsdon, R. G., & Teri, L. (1997). The Pleasant Events Schedule-AD: Psychometric properties and relationship to depression and cognition in Alzheimer's disease patients. *Gerontologist, 37*(1), 40–45.

Lustbader, W. (2004). *What's worth knowing.* New York: Simon & Schuster.

Lustbader, W. (1993). *Counting on kindness: The dilemmas of dependency.* New York: Simon & Schuster.

Mace, N. L., & Rabins, P. V. (1981). *The 36-hour day: A family guide to caring for persons with Alzheimer's disease, related dementing illnesses and memory loss in later life.* Baltimore: Johns Hopkins University Press.

Mahoney, D. F., Tarlow, B. J., & Jones, R. N. (2003). Effects of an automated telephone support system on caregiver burden and anxiety: Findings from the REACH for TLC intervention study. *Gerontologist, 43*(4), 556–567.

Martin-Cook, K., Remakel-Davis, B., Svetlik, D., Hynan, L. S., & Weiner, M. F. (2003). Caregiver attribution and resentment in dementia care. *American Journal of Alzheimer's Disease and Other Dementias, 18*(6), 366–374.

McCormick, W., Kukull, W., van Belle, G., Bowen, J., Teri, L., & Larson, E. (1995). The effects of diagnosing Alzheimer's disease on frequency of physician visits. *Journal of General Internal Medicine, 10*(4), 187–193.

McCurry, S. M., Gibbons, L. E., Logsdon, R. G., Vitiello, M. V., & Teri, L. (1995). Nighttime Insomnia Treatment and Education for Alzheimer's Disease (NITE-AD): A randomized controlled trial. *Journal of the American Geriatrics Society, 53*(5), 793–802.

McCurry, S. M., Logsdon, R. G., Vitiello, M. V., & Teri, L. (1998). Successful behavioral treatment for reported sleep problems in elderly caregivers of dementia patients: A controlled study. *Journal of Gerontology: Psychological Sciences, 53B*(3), P122–P129.

McCurry, S. M., & Teri, L. (1997). Advance planning in dementia caregivers. *Journal of the American Geriatrics Society, 45*(9), 1102–1103.

McCurry, S. M., Vitiello, M. V., Gibbons, L. E., Logsdon, R. G., & Teri, L. (in press). Factors associated with caregiver perceptions of sleep disturbances in persons with dementia. *American Journal of Geriatric Psychiatry.*

Mittelman, M. S., Roth, D. L., Haley, W. E., & Zarit, S. H. (2004). Effects of a caregiver intervention on negative caregiver appraisals of behavior problems in patients with Alzheimer's disease: Results of a randomized trial. *Journal of Gerontology: Psychological Sciences, 59B*(1), P27–P34.

Mizuno, E., Hosak, T., Ogihara, R., Higano, H., & Mano, Y. (1999). Effectiveness of a stress management program for family caregivers of the elderly at home. *Journal of Medicine and Dental Science, 46*(4), 145–153.

Murphy, E. M., & Clark, D. M. (1998). *Laughter among the tears: Living with Alzheimer's*. Shawnee, OK: Fly Away Press.

Neuringer, A. (2004). Reinforced variability in animals and people: Implications for adaptive action. *American Psychologist, 59*(9), 891–906.

Nolan, M., Ingram, P., & Watson, R. (2003). Caring for people with dementia: Working together to enhance caregiver coping and support. In M. Nolan, U. Lundh, G. Grant, & J. Keady (Eds.), *Partnerships in family care* (pp. 128–144). Philadelphia: Open University Press.

Nolan, M., Ryan, T., Enderby, P., & Reid, D. (2002). Toward a more inclusive vision of dementia care practice and research. *Dementia, 1*(2), 192–211.

Patterson, C. J., Gauthier, S., Bergman, H., Cohen, C. A., Feightner, J. W., Feldman, H., et al. (1999). The recognition, assessment and management of dementing disorders: Conclusions from the Canadian Consensus Conference on Dementia. *Canadian Medical Association Journal, 160*(Suppl. 12), S1–S15.

Paun, O. (2004). Female Alzheimer's patient caregivers share their strength. *Holistic Nursing Practice, 18*(1), 11–17.

Pinquart, M., & Sorensen, S. (2004). Associations of caregiver stressors and uplifts with subjective well-being and depressive mood: A meta-analytic comparison. *Aging and Mental Health, 8*(5), 438–449.

Pinquart, M., & Sorensen, S. (2003a). Associations of stressors and uplifts of caregiving with caregiver burden and depressive mood: A meta-analysis. *Journal of Gerontology: Psychological Sciences, 58B*(2), P112–P128.

Pinquart, M., & Sorensen, S. (2003b). Differences between caregivers and non-caregivers in psychological health and physical health: A meta-analysis. *Psychology and Aging, 18*(2), 250–267.

Price, A. (2004). Encouraging reflection and critical thinking in practice. *Nursing Standard, 18*(47), 46–54.

Prochaska, J. O., DiClemente, C. C., & Norcross, J. C. (1992). In search of how people change: Applications to addictive behaviors. *American Psychologist, 47*(9), 1102–1114.

Rader, J., & Tornquist, E. M. (1995). *Individualized dementia care: Creative, compassionate approaches*. New York: Springer Publishing.

The Random House Dictionary of the English Language. (1966). Unabridged edition. New York: Random House.

Reifler, B. V. (1995). What I want if I get Alzheimer's disease. *Archives of Family Medicine, 4*(5), 395–396.

Reimer, M. A., Slaughter, S., Donaldson, C., Currie, G., & Eliaziw, M. (2004). Special care facility compared with traditional environments for dementia care: A longitudinal study of quality of life. *Journal of the American Geriatrics Society, 52*(7), 1085–1092.

Reynolds, D. K. (1989). *Flowing bridges, quiet waters: Japanese psychotherapies, Morita and Naikan*. Albany: State University of New York Press.

Richards, K. C., Sullivan, S. C., Phillips, R. L., Beck, C. K., & Overton-McCoy, A. L. (2001). The effect of individualized activities on the sleep of nursing home residents who are cognitively impaired: A pilot study. *Journal of Gerontological Nursing, 27*(9), 30–37.

Riegel, K. F. (1975). Toward a dialectical theory of development. *Human Development, 18*, 50–64.

Roberts, D. C., & Cleveland, L. A. (2001). Surrounded by ocean, a world apart . . . The experience of women living alone. *Holistic Nurse Nursing Practice, 15*(3), 45–55.

Rosen, C. S., Chow, H. C., Greenbaum, M. A., Finney, J. F., Moos, R. H., Sheikh, J. I., et al. (2002). How well are clinicians following dementia practice guidelines? *Alzheimer Disease and Associated Disorders, 16*(1), 15–23.

Rosso, J., Lukins, S., & McLaughlin, M. (1979). *The silver palate cookbook*. New York: Workman Publishing.

Rutter, M. (1985). Resilience in the face of adversity: Protective factors and resistance to psychiatric disorder. *British Journal of Psychiatry, 147*(6), 598–611.

Sacks, O. (1998). *The man who mistook his wife for a hat: And other clinical tales*. New York: Simon & Schuster.

Samples, P., Larsen, D., & Larsen, M. (2000). *Selfcare for caregivers: A twelve step approach*. Center City, MN: Hazelden Publishing & Educational Services.

Schulz, R. & Martire, L. M. (2004). Family caregiving of persons with dementia: Prevalence, health effects, and support strategies. *American Journal of Geriatric Psychiatry, 13*(3), 240–249.

Shapiro, E. R. (2002). Chronic illness as a family process: A social-developmental approach to promoting resilience. *Journal of Clinical Psychology, 58*(11), 1375–1384.

Small, J. A., & Gutman, G. (2002). Recommended and reported use of communication strategies in Alzheimer caregiving. *Alzheimer Disease and Associated Disorders, 16*(4), 270–278.

Snow, I. A., Hovanec, L., & Brandt, J. (2004). A controlled trial of aromatherapy for agitation in nursing home patients with dementia. *Journal of Alternative and Complementary Medicine, 10*(3), 431–437.

Teri, L., Gibbons, L. E., McCurry, S. M., Logsdon, R. G., Buchner, D. M., Barlow, W. E., et al. (2003). Exercise plus behavioral management in patients with Alzheimer disease: A randomized controlled trial. *Journal of the American Medical Association, 290*(15), 2015–2022.

Teri, L., & Logsdon, R. G. (2000). Assessment and management of behavioral disturbances in Alzheimer disease. *Comprehensive Therapy, 26*(3), 171–175.

Teri, L., & Logsdon, R. G. (1991). Identifying pleasant activities for Alzheimer's disease patients: The Pleasant Events Schedule-AD. *Gerontologist, 31*(1), 124–127.

Teri, L., Logsdon, R. G., & McCurry, S. M. (2005). The Seattle Protocols: Advances in behavioral treatment of Alzheimer's disease. In B. Vellas, L. J. Fitten, B. Winblad, H. Feldman, M. Grundman, & E. Giacobini (Eds.), *Research and practice in Alzheimer's disease and cognitive decline* (pp. 153–158). Paris: Serdi Publisher.

Teri, L., Logsdon, R. G., & McCurry, S. M. (2002). Nonpharmacological treatment of behavioral disturbance in dementia. *The Medical Clinics of North America, 86*(3), 641–656.

Teri, L., Logsdon, R. G., Uomoto, J., & McCurry, S. (1997). Behavioral treatment of depression in dementia patients: A controlled clinical trial. *Journal of Gerontology: Psychological Sciences, 52B*(4), P159–P166.

Teri, L., Logsdon, R. G., Whall, A. L., Weiner, M. F., Trimmer, C., Peskind, E., et al. (1998). Treatment for agitation in dementia patients: A behavior management approach. *Psychotherapy, 35*(4), 436–443.

Teri, L., McCurry, S. M., Logsdon, R. G., & Gibbons, L. E. (in press). Training community consultants to help family members improve dementia care: A randomized controlled trial. *Gerontologist.*

Teri, L., McCurry, S. M., Logsdon, R. G., Huda, P., & Korkowski, A. (2003). *Treatment of depression and anxiety in persons with dementia.* Treatment manual. Seattle: University of Washington.

Teri, L., & Piruz, H. (2002). *S.T.A.R.: Staff training in assisted living residences.* Training manual. Seattle: University of Washington.

Thorgrimsen, L., Spector, A., Wiles, A., & Orrell, M. (2003). Aroma therapy for dementia. *Cochrane Database of Systematic Reviews,* 2003(3):CD003150.

Tune, L. E. (2001). Anticholinergic effects of medication in elderly patients. *Journal of Clinical Psychiatry, 62*(Suppl. 21), 11–14.

Tusaie, K., & Dyer, J. (2004). Resilience: A historical review of the construct. *Holistic Nursing Practice, 18*(1), 3–8.

Vink, A. C., Birks, J. S., Bruinsma, M. S., & Scholten, R. J. (2004). Music therapy for people with dementia. *Cochrane Database of Systematic Reviews,* 2004(3): CD003477.

Vitaliano, P. P., Zhang, J., & Scanlan, J. M. (2003). Is caregiving hazardous to one's physical health? A meta-analysis. *Psychological Bulletin, 129*(6), 946–972.

Waelde, L. C., Thompson, L., & Gallagher-Thompson, D. (2004). A pilot study of a yoga and meditation intervention for dementia caregiver stress. *Journal of Clinical Psychology, 60*(6), 677–687.

Wagnild, G. (2003). Resilience and successful aging: Comparison among low and high income older adults. *Journal of Gerontological Nursing, 29*(12), 42–49.

Wagnild, G., & Young, H. M. (1990). Resilience among older women. *Image: Journal of Nursing Scholarship, 22*(4), 252–255.

Wagnild, G., & Young, H. M. (1993). Development and psychometric evaluation of the resilience scale. *Journal of Nursing Measurement, 1*(2), 165–178.

Wasserman, E. A., Young, M. E., & Cook, R. G. (2004). Variability discrimination in humans and animals. *American Psychologist, 59*(9), 879–890.

Wilcox, E. W. (1919). *Poems by Ella Wheeler Wilcox*. Toronto: McClelland & Stewart.

Williamson, G. M., & Shaffer, D. R. (2001). Relationship quality and potentially harmful behaviors by spousal caregivers: How we were then, how we are now. The Family Relationships in Late Life Project. *Psychology and Aging, 16*(2), 217–226.

Young, H. M., & de Tornyay, R. (2001). *Choices: Making a good move to a retirement community*. Seattle, WA: ERA Care Communities.

Index

About the Author

SUSAN M. McCURRY is Research Associate Professor in the Department of Psychosocial and Community Health and Adjunct Research Associate Professor in the Department of Psychiatry and Behavioral Sciences at the University of Washington and an attending psychologist in the Geriatric and Family Services Clinic in the U.W. Internal Medicine Department.